# HAVE THE SEX YOU WANT

## Also by Andrew G. Marshall

*I Love You but I'm Not in Love with You:*
*Seven Steps to Saving Your Relationship*

*I Love You but You Always Put Me Last:*
*Why the Kids-First Approach to Parenting Is Hurting Your*
*Marriage—and the Proven Plan to Restore Balance*

*My Wife Doesn't Love Me Anymore:*
*The Love Coach Guide to Winning Her Back*

*Learn to Love Yourself Enough: Seven Steps to*
*Improving Your Self-Esteem and Your Relationships*

*How Can I Ever Trust You Again?*
*Infidelity from Discovery to Recovery in Seven Steps*

*Heal and Move On: Seven Steps to Recovering*
*from a Breakup*

*Help Your Partner Say "Yes": Seven Steps to*
*Achieving Better Cooperation and Communication*

*Resolve Your Differences: Seven Steps*
*to Dealing with Conflict in Your Relationship*

*Are You Right for Me? Seven Steps to*
*Getting Clarity and Commitment in Your Relationship*

# HAVE THE
# SEX
# YOU WANT

## A Couple's Guide
## to Getting Back the Spark

### ANDREW G. MARSHALL

MARSHALL METHOD
PUBLISHING

The case histories in this book are based on couples with whom I have worked in my marital therapy practice (their identities have been changed to protect confidentiality and sometimes two or three cases have been merged together) and individuals who wrote to my website, filled in a questionnaire or kept a sex diary.

If readers have a medical complaint, it is important that they consult their doctor.

**Marshall Method Publishing**
London • Florida
www.marshallmethodpublishing.com

**Library of Congress Cataloging-in-Publication Data is available through the Library of Congress.**

This work has been previously been published in the UK (Bloomsbury) as *Make Love Like a Prairie Vole: Six Steps to Passionate, Plentiful and Monogamous Sex.*

ISBN 978-0-9574297-9-6

Editor: Michele Matrisciani
Cover and interior design: Gary A. Rosenberg

Printed in the United States of America

10  9  8  7  6  5  4  3  2  1

# Contents

# Introduction

Sex plays a central part in our lives. It not only makes us feel desirable and loved, but an orgasm is a great physical release and a reducer of stress. Most important of all, sex bonds us to our partners and stops our relationships from disintegrating into friendship or one strictly of co-parenting. Unfortunately, sex is also difficult to discuss with our partners . . . *especially* with our partners. Even an innocent discussion of what we enjoy can be interpreted as criticism. The whole topic is so full of traps that most couples retreat into silence and hope for the best.

That's fine at the beginning of the relationship when everything is new and exciting, but what happens several years down the road when sex has become predictable and there's always something else demanding your attention?

Although you've both changed over the years, you're probably still having the same sex as when you first met. However, you are probably not going to the same restaurants, wearing the same clothes, and listening to the same music, so it's no wonder the spark has gone out of your love life, leaving you both bored and a little frustrated. Despite the media's being full of titillation, there is no serious discussion of how to keep passion alive in long-term relationships. Of course, there are books offering "sex tips," which can be useful if you're looking for a superficial fix, but they don't assist in figuring out what has gone awry and why, and most important, what to do about it.

As a marital therapist with close to thirty years of couples counseling experience, I have witnessed this phenomenon over and over again in

1

Have the Sex You Want

clients of all ages and stages of their relationships, and I am here to tell you that you don't have to settle for infrequent or "going through the motions" lovemaking. You *can* have the sex you want: passionate, plentiful, and connected. In this book, I show you how to talk to your partner about sex without fighting, how to understand the myths that undermine good lovemaking, and most important, how to be more sensual and "in the moment," so you forget your everyday concerns, completely let go, and—having stepped away from your to-do list—bask in the joy of fulfilling sex.

It sounds wonderful, doesn't it? Except you're skeptical. Do your problems seem too deep to uncover or your partner so defensive, uninterested in sex, or just plain angry to the point where you can't fathom ever connecting with him or her the way you used to? Don't worry; I've come across all these problems before, and I'm here as a guide and a source for everything you want to know and need to know about reigniting the spark.

The first three chapters focus on improving communication and repairing damage done to your relationship through years of shutting each other out, humiliation, misunderstanding, mismatched libido, over-scheduled lives, or any other culprit that caused a gap in your connection. In Chapter Four, I introduce my ten-week program that defies "logic," by stripping your lovemaking back to basics and unlearning any bad habits that are driving you apart. By adhering to the "no sex" rule, you will relearn how to turn your partner on, set your fantasies free, and introduce new ideas that could spice up your lovemaking. In the last two chapters, I offer a lens into the problems of sexual functioning and unresolved issues, including affairs and sex addiction. The book concludes with a recap of the ten-week program along with advice, if you're reading this book alone, on how to recruit your partner to change your sex life.

You will probably discover that your partner has been lying on the opposite side of the bed feeling just as frustrated as you are, which means there is hope for not just better sex but making a fresh start too.

# Chapter One

# The Six Stages of Lovemaking

Exchanging loaded looks, the building of desire, the intimate touch, the lingering kisses as two people give up control and surrender to each other, we have a clear picture of really good sex. For a few blissful moments, you are not alone but united in giving and receiving pleasure. In your lover's eyes, you have become supremely desirable and that makes you feel powerful and at peace with yourself. At the same time, you're offering the same gift to your lover. All your everyday problems melt away as the feelings build and build into a long and satisfying climax. Afterward, you lie in each other's arms as your breathing slowly returns to normal, leaving you in a blissful state.

But, for many, sex seems to be the last thought of two tired people at the end of a long day. Of course, it can still be wonderful, but that tends to happen when you're on vacation and you're relaxed and making time for each other. For the other fifty weeks of the year, instead of being something that bonds you and makes life worth living, sex becomes another thing on your to-do list, a source of arguments, or an altogether off-limits topic.

What happened to that spark that drew you together? What happened to the passion you thought would last forever?

The good news is that sex does not have to go from a tidal wave of lust —sweeping all before it—to a gush and then a trickle. It flows through six different stages, each with its own pleasures, problems, and rewards. Unfortunately, films, novels, and pop songs celebrate lovemaking at the beginning of a relationship, leaving us to guess the rest of the story.

# UNDERSTANDING LOVEMAKING IN SIX STAGES

Sex means different things and has different jobs in your relationship at different points along your journey together. Understanding your stage and its particular challenges is the key to passionate and plentiful love-making. This will keep you from worrying that every snag is caused by a fundamental problem and provide the wisdom to know when an issue requires serious attention.

## STAGE 1—Lust (Zero to Six Months)

> *"Lust is actually very inward looking, meaning it is more about us and our personal fantasies than the other person."*

Lust narrows the distance between us and an attractive stranger, or else we would never muster the courage to cross the room and say hello, and it provides the impetus to turn an acquaintance or friend into something more. Without lust's power, it is doubtful that we'd have the nerve to get naked, touch each other, and fuse our bodies together.

Lust provided the urge for Jeff, twenty-five, to pursue his future wife. "I used to park my motorcycle at a friend's garage. On this occasion, my friend wasn't there, but his new roommate, Susan, answered the door. She invited me in for coffee, and we sat in the kitchen and talked and talked. All the time, I hoped my friend wouldn't come back because I knew he was interested in her too. My tongue would be talking about the weather or something, but my brain would be thinking, *How can I get her?*"

Women are just as responsive to lust as men, although they have traditionally been the gatekeepers to sex and supposedly less under its spell. "This fireman dropped by the office where I work. He'd been looking for the building supervisor. He smiled, and I literally felt light headed and giggly," explained Samantha, thirty-one. "He stayed by my desk a moment longer than necessary and I asked his name, so I could tell the supervisor who'd been looking for him—nothing more, honest. When he left, I ran around to the front of the building, which looks over the parking lot, to see if he'd brought his fire engine. Disappointingly, he hadn't.

At just that moment, he looked up and we made eye contact. Perhaps it was the uniform, perhaps it was pure lust, but I felt compelled to wave. Instead of getting into his car, he strode across the car park, came back upstairs, and asked me out for Friday night. We spent the whole weekend in bed."

Although there may be a strong physical connection with the object of our desire and the possibility of an emotional connection too, lust is actually very inward looking, meaning it is more about us and our personal fantasies than the other person. Looking back on her weekend of hot sex, Samantha admitted that it had been more about her desire to be rescued (her divorce had just been finalized) than laying down the foundations for a relationship.

For Jeff, however, the bike ride was the beginning of a three-year courtship with Susan. "She was completely different from anybody I'd ever met. It was exciting, and I was living on pure adrenaline. Her father hated me, thought I was a loser. We came from different worlds. Could she love me back?"

### The Catch

Lust makes us blind to both the weaknesses and the strengths of a budding relationship. At one end of the scale, it can bind two totally unsuitable people together. At the other, when lust wears off, two lovers with a perfectly viable future will start to doubt their judgment.

## STAGE 2—Bonding (Six Months to Three Years)

*"Two people's individual sexuality is fused
into a couple's sensuality."*

While lust is all about claiming and possessing, however fleetingly, the other person, this next stage is about building a durable relationship. Instead of your beloved being a walking, breathing, sighing embodiment of your fantasies, he or she is emerging as a real person. Sex can also become more complicated, as two people's individual *sexuality* (how someone likes to be touched, what turns him on, whether she is more sexually responsive at night or in the morning) is fused into a couple's *sensuality* (what a couple enjoys doing together).

Sheena, thirty-two, had been so swept away with the passion of her early lovemaking to Christopher, thirty-one, that she had been carried over some of her personal boundaries. "I'm not really comfortable about being touched in intimate places," she explained on her first session. Like many people, Sheena did not have the words to discuss sex and used a variety of euphemisms or dropped hints hoping that Christopher would understand. (For more on talking about sex, see Lexicon for Lovemaking in Sex Ed at the end of this chapter.)

I asked Sheena a few questions and identified that although she had agreed to oral sex at the beginning of the relationship, she had changed her mind. "I didn't mind so much to start off. It felt nice, and I didn't want to upset Christopher, but when I'd had a chance to think, I wasn't so sure," she explained. Meanwhile, Christopher was not only unaware of these reservations but also hadn't realized that she had not enjoyed giving him oral sex.

Fortunately, Sheena's feelings about oral sex did not prevent the couple from bonding. After all, as Christopher said, "There are plenty of other things we enjoy in the bedroom."

### The Catch

Some people find that the closer they bond to their beloved, the less they desire them. It is almost as if they have separated love and desire. Some couples discover that once lust has worn off (along with the overwhelming need to physically possess the other person), it is harder to find a way from their everyday life together into the sensual world of lovemaking.

### STAGE 3—Settled (Three+ Years)

> *"At this stage, sex is about making us feel complete as human beings."*

While lust is based on surprise, the unknown, and novelty, settled sex is about security, comfort, and stability. While bonding sex is about spanning the distance between the "me" of two individuals into the "we" of an established relationship and discovering the real person behind the fantasy (which can be a source of anxiety), settled sex is reassuring and safe.

On one hand, it is good to be able to relax and worry less about what our partner thinks. Sheena, for example, started to allow Christopher to leave the light on while they made love. "I know he loves me and accepts me, so I've started to worry less about how I look."

Christopher was also able to admit to his body issues: "I stopped leaving my T-shirt on when we went to the beach to hide my love handles and didn't think I had to hold my breath in the whole time I made love."

In the settled stage, previous negotiation and conflict over what will be and not be part of your lovemaking is replaced by an acceptance of what you do both enjoy and a greater knowledge of each other's bodies. However, this sense of security and being sure of each other can easily turn into taking each other for granted. Instead of setting aside time for your erotic needs, it is easy to demote them and prioritize cleaning the kitchen, checking emails, or watching TV.

At this stage, sex is about making us feel complete as human beings. Imagine a spectrum with "control" at one end and "surrender" at the other. Modern life stresses the importance of taking charge of our destiny, and technological advances offer us the opportunity for more and more control over our environment. Meanwhile, we have downgraded surrender to an afterthought, a luxury or something that can only be enjoyed after earning a living, getting a pension, and doing chores. However, control and surrender are equally important, and sex is one of the few places where these two different needs can be reconciled.

Strangely enough, the best way to illustrate how control and surrender can coexist is to look at the history of shipbuilding. Wooden ships had to be regularly taken out of the water and patched to stop them from leaking. When technology improved, it became possible to make ships that didn't expand and shrink as much as the wooden ones. In theory, greater control over what happened to the ships in the water and under different weather conditions should have been a huge step forward. Except these new ships were disasters. They were too rigid. Under stress, they would crack apart. So boat builders went back to ships that didn't quite fit; ships that could flex. In effect, the best vessels *surrendered* to their environment and allowed themselves to be moved by the power of the sea. No wonder with our current emphasis on control and refusal to surrender that so many of us have mental breakdowns or are floored by depression, anxiety, and compulsive disorders.

Our grandparents' generation had the benefit of being religious, and faith offers many opportunities for surrender, either by giving up control to a higher power or through communal worship (where each member of the congregation is no longer an individual but part of something bigger). Even though many people today are no longer churchgoers, they still need to step away from their everyday life and have a moment of transcendence. Perhaps it is not surprising that our society often faces an increase in alcohol and drug abuse, as these offer temporary but dysfunctional ways of letting go.

There are, however, less damaging ways to surrender. The first is through art, whether creating it or observing it. From singing in a choir and playing in a band to dancing with a troupe to joining a writers' group, people can use artistic expression to submerge into something greater than themselves. They can also be carried away and forget their own lives for a while by identifying with the characters in a good book or film. The second source of surrender is in the act of making love because you can put aside everyday trivia, enjoy an orgasm, and, having stepped away from the modern mania of feeling in control (if only for a few minutes), bask in the joy of feeling completely connected to another person.

### The Catch

Settled lovemaking can easily go from feeling safe to predictable once anticipation and passion head out the door. There is an added danger by this stage in your relationship: You imagine that you know everything about your partner (closing your eyes to his or her true complexity and only seeing what reinforces your own idea of that person). Worse, we can imagine our partner's character and tastes are fixed and therefore believe change is impossible.

## STAGE 4—Parenting

*"With all the emotions closer to the surface,*
*couples can grow closer and bond more deeply,*
*even if making love happens less frequently than before."*

Although the first three stages depend on how long you've been together, the next three are affected by your circumstances and your age.

Couples who meet in their late thirties or early forties, when a woman's biological clock might be ticking at its loudest, will often try to get pregnant almost immediately (and find themselves with the additional focus of bonding as a couple as well as coping with being new parents). Meanwhile, couples who meet after child-rearing years will skip this stage altogether.

For the majority of couples, however, who have known each other for three or more years and have safely moved through the lust, bonding, and settled sex stages, deciding to have a baby can empower their sex lives. Now, there's no longer any worry about getting pregnant, and the biological drive for a baby can make for lusty lovemaking. No wonder both men and women often look back at this time with fond memories. Becoming pregnant can also boost a woman's self-confidence, self-esteem, and sense of femininity. I've counseled many women who have finally made peace with their bodies, enjoying their new curves and reveling in the miracle of creation, especially if they had teenage eating disorders, self-harmed, or were sexually abused. Some men find their partner's bump and the proof of their own fertility a turn-on. With all the emotions closer to the surface, couples can grow closer and bond more deeply, even if making love happens less frequently than before.

Unfortunately, the opposite can also be true. Infertility issues can transform lovemaking from an adventure into a chore. After conception, some couples worry about harming the baby during sex (not a problem unless there is a history of miscarriage, low-lying placenta, bleeding, or a cervical weakness). In addition, morning sickness, the problems of finding a comfortable position in bed for lovemaking, and the general messiness of pregnancy can take their toll. In a survey of 3,000 mothers-to-be, 40 percent found it difficult to feel sexy and 20 percent were convinced their partners had lost all desire for them (Babywebsite.com 2008). For some men, watching their partner give birth and breast feed can have a serious effect on their libido, as her vagina and breasts are transformed from fun to functional.

Mike, forty-two, and Jenny, thirty-five, found sex went from "exciting" to "just get it over with" after their daughter was born. By the time they decided to come for counseling, their child was three, and Mike was feeling so unloved and undesirable that he had threatened to move out. Not surprisingly, Jenny felt under attack.

"I'm trying my best, but when Mike comes at me all hands, it can be a bit overwhelming. I was never cuddled as a child, so I can find that sort of intimacy tough."

Mike cut in, "You should be flattered that I still find you so attractive."

Their sex life had deteriorated after a miscarriage five months before. Unfortunately, they had not really talked about this experience together, and Mike was not aware that Jenny still had feelings of grief.

They were also suffering from the common problem of hormonally affected libido. After a woman gives birth, and for about eighteen months afterward in typical cases, an increase in levels of oxytocin, known as the "bonding hormone," causes the woman to divert her attention away from her partner (or anything else for that matter) and tend to her child. This is particularly problematic when couples have more than one child under the age of five, as not only are both parents exhausted, but the woman's hormones might only have just begun to recover. Mike thought that Jenny's lack of interest was personal. "I think she is no longer attracted to me, so what's the point of carrying on?"

## The Catch

Babies bring out the protective side in everybody. We want to hold them, hug them, and bounce them on our knee. We blow onto their bellies and nibble their toes. They smell wonderful. Just handling a baby, changing their diapers, and caring for them provides lots of skin-on-skin contact. No wonder some women say they're not interested in sex—the bond with their baby is providing all the validation and human contact that normally comes from sex.

## STAGE 5—Personal Reinvention

*"The increased confidence that comes with getting older and a better sense of who we are makes us less likely to do what is expected of us and likelier to do what is right for us."*

For most people, personal reinvention happens around forty years old, but it can be anywhere between thirty-five and fifty. The increased confidence that comes with getting older and a better sense of who we are makes us less likely to do what is expected of us and likelier to do what is right for us. Naturally, this confidence spills over into our sex lives, and many people find new ways of expressing themselves. Hopefully, these changes are done as a couple, but if communication has broken down or someone views his or her wife or husband as an obstacle rather than a partner for change, this can be a time of affairs and relationship breakdown. Even in the best relationships, there are challenges and worries. The compromises forged during the bonding stage—when a couple created a joint sexuality of what they enjoyed together—need to be revisited and refreshed. After all, however pleasurable lovemaking might be, if it is performed in the same way, over and over again without any changes, the shine is bound to wear thin.

Paul, forty-two, had always been a gentle and considerate lover and that was perfect for Susie, thirty-nine, when they first met in their early twenties. "I was just out of college, shy, and anxious. I'd had one or two boyfriends, nothing serious. So it was important that Paul took his time and really wooed me, but I'm no longer that person."

Susie had worked hard, gotten a promotion, and headed up a team of six people. "They're always coming to me and asking, 'Should I do this?' or 'What about that?' So when Paul and I are lying in bed and he asks, 'What can I do for you?' I want to scream, and not with passion!"

"So what kind of lovemaking would you like?" I asked.

"I want him to be forceful, take charge," she replied.

I could tell she wanted to say something more, so I nodded my head encouragingly.

"I have this fantasy where this burglar breaks into the house and pleasures me in a hundred different ways."

11

"And that makes you feel desired and sexy? A grown-up woman who cannot only take care of herself but reduce an intruder to a quivering wreck, in the best sense of the word?" I asked.

"Why didn't you tell me?" Paul looked at her with a certain relief.

Susie was embarrassed, partly about confessing her secret fantasy and partly at how hard it had been to tell her husband that she wanted to mix things up.

They returned the next week wreathed in smiles.

"It was great to take charge, let myself go," said Paul. "None of my normal dropping hints or wheedling for sex. I ordered her to strip. When we started making out, I was worried that I might be hurting her or being disrespectful, but Susie was moaning with pleasure."

Again, I could tell he wanted to say something more. He looked shyly at Susie.

"In my head, I was that burglar, enjoying myself and not caring what she thought."

## The Catch

Our fears about aging and loss of sexual potency often tip the reinvention phase of lovemaking from a difficult bump in the road into a complete block. Many people jump out of a perfectly good relationship terrified that this is their last chance for happiness. Ironically, they end up leaving at the moment when the best lovemaking is just within their reach.

## STAGE 6—Glory Days

*"The great advantage of being older is that you are less likely to be trying to prove yourself."*

If you have successfully negotiated your midlife personal reinvention, you're ready to reap the benefits, especially if you and your partner have been together for twenty-five years or more (and have *really* gotten to know each other). For couples who meet later in life, and are perhaps in their second marriages, the opportunity to explore sexuality with someone new can be liberating and confidence-building.

Contrary to popular belief, sex is not just for the young, beautiful, and virile. For truly satisfying lovemaking, you need to bring the whole of your personality, not just your genitals, so the extra self-knowledge that comes with age and experience is a real asset. That's why many of my clients in their fifties and beyond are having the best sex of their lives.

The great advantage of being older is that you are less likely to be trying to prove yourself. Sex is simply a source of pleasure rather than a way of bolstering your ego or getting reassurance. While previously the focus has been outward—career, nest building, and child rearing—time and energy can now be devoted to each other, and sex no longer has to be the last thought of two exhausted people.

James, fifty-one, had been a high-flying lawyer but decided to scale back to a less pressured job. "When I was growing up, I had a deep fear of things not going right. I couldn't just pass the exam, I had to come out at the top of my class. This fear of failure and desire to impress other people carried over into my career. I'd be away a lot. My marriage suffered because I was always exhausted or working, even on weekends. I missed the first half of my fortieth birthday weekend in Antigua because I was closing a deal in London. I just attached so much importance to everything, because if I didn't get it right, there was this incredible doom looming behind it."

It took the death of his father, a similarly driven man, for James to stop and take stock. "I realized I hardly knew my father. I was angry because he'd cut himself off from everybody. Nobody knew him. Then it hit me: sitting by his hospital bed, I was looking at myself twenty years down the line, or maybe less, the way I was working."

So how had this revelation affected James's love life?

"I don't try to live up to the expectations of being the best at work or at play, and ironically when I stopped trying, I had this huge weight lifted off my shoulders, and I started to enjoy sex more. I don't know what my wife thinks, but I think it's brought us much closer."

His wife, Marie, agrees. "Before, sex was fine, but I always felt like it was another thing he had to check off his list, like going for a run or catching up on emails. Now he's actually one hundred percent with me, and that makes everything that much deeper, more connected. The other

13

night, after we made love, he cried, and I held him in my arms. I asked him what was wrong."

James took back the story. "All these dark feelings came up, all these regrets. Why had I put so much energy into pleasing everybody but the very people who really counted?"

"You're here now and that's what counts." Marie took his hand.

They were truly in the glory days of their relationship.

Growing older for Donna has been liberating, and, in her late forties, she is having better sex than ever before. "I feel free in my body. It might not be so nice to look at, but I've stopped worrying about what I might look like from this or that angle, and that's wonderful. I would definitely say I'm enjoying myself more today than twenty-something sex, when I felt under pressure to do what was supposed to be exciting (like dressing up) and what my husband expected (like groaning at all the right times) rather than what I wanted."

But as Donna admitted, at that age, she had no idea what she wanted outside the bedroom, so what chance did she have of expressing her true sexuality? "I feel very safe in my relationship. My second husband and I have been together for twenty years, and we know each other inside out. The kids are grown, life is less of a struggle, and a lot of my friends are reporting the same thing. They're feeling much more in the mood. It took me until this age, but I'm finally into sex. I look at it as a gift from mother nature."

While some people think familiarity breeds boredom, the opposite has been true for Donna. "I feel able to experiment, push my boundaries, and try different things, like playing with toys and trying different positions, which my twenty-something self would have thought disgusting and perverted, but which I find really exciting."

Richard, fifty-one, is embarrassed to admit to some of his twenty-something hang-ups. "I thought men should be in charge in the bedroom, so when my girlfriend started writhing under me during intercourse, thrusting up to meet me, I thought that's my job and would stop until she was still again. How stupid is that? She was really enjoying herself and instead of reveling in how she could lose herself in the pleasure of the moment, I was worrying she might guess that she was my first lover. In those days, I don't think we ever really connected because I was an insecure control freak."

"I was brought up to be very goal orientated," says Philip, fifty-five. "I spent so much time trying to influence things that couldn't be changed." Fortunately, he had stopped being so outcome-focused, and this had revolutionized his sex life.

"I felt I *had* to give my wife an orgasm, and if I didn't have one also, it meant I was a terrible failure. So I'd stay over on my side of the bed, unless I was certain I'd deliver. Now, our lovemaking is more leisurely, more cuddles and less goals. It's so much better."

## The Catch

If a couple has not mixed up their lovemaking during the reinvention stage, it is likely that one or both partners will be bored. Often, in counseling, one partner will admit to being afraid of showing his or her inner lustiness for fear of being judged or rejected, only to find that his or her partner has similar inhibitions. A double bind ensues, and it's hard to let go with someone who is buttoned up.

## SOMETHING TO SLEEP ON

In summary, remember:

- To improve the overall quality of your sex life, it is important to understand how lovemaking evolves over time and whether problems are part of a natural transition from one stage to another or something more serious.

- The ease of sex during the lust phase (claiming and possessing) can blind us to the more complex lovemaking of the bonding, settled, and parenting phases.

- During the reinvention phase (taking a fresh look at the compromises made, possibly years earlier during the previous three stages), it is easy to believe time is running out and that this is the last chance for sexual happiness, thereby increasing the likelihood of affairs and relationship breakdown.

- Couples who learn from the reinvention phase reap the benefit of "glory days" sex when each partner brings a greater knowledge of who they are, rather than just their genitals, to lovemaking.

# SEX ED

## EXERCISE 1   WORK ON YOUR STAGE OF LOVEMAKING

How long you and your partner have been together has a big impact on your sex life and the types of problems that you might face. Try these tips for your particular lovemaking stage.

### LUST: The First Six Months

The first few months of a new relationship should be full of easy and enjoyable sex. However, I counsel some people who are worried they are not feeling passionate enough and wonder if something is wrong. Of course, it may be that you and your new boyfriend or girlfriend are simply incompatible, but if you care enough to pick up this book, the answer probably lies deeper. In my experience, most cases of inhibited libido come down to fear. Therefore, lack of passion in this stage could indicate:

✗ Performance anxiety (*Am I skilled or attractive enough?*).

✗ Baggage from a previous relationship.

✗ Believing the soul-mate myth.

So what is the soul-mate myth and how does it affect fledgling sexual relationships? Soul mates are supposed to connect on such a fundamental level and share so many tastes and interests that all differences, problems, and obstacles somehow melt away. Both partners feel completely understood and look forward to a life of total bliss together. Of course, you need a connection to make a good relationship, but more important, you also need skills: The ability to say what you need (rather than expect your partner to know) and to negotiate and compromise when your needs clash with your partner's (rather than hoping to always agree).

However, if you never saw your parents communicate effectively, whether it's because they were always fighting, disappointing each other, or sulking, you will not have learned these skills yourself. Worse, you might have had a ringside view of just how destructive these behaviors can be to a marriage. No wonder you are determined to avoid the same traps, which is why the idea of soul mates is so appealing: all you need to do is find *the one*.

If this illusion were true, then sex at the beginning of a relationship should not just be "okay" (with the hope that as you get to know each other it will improve), but off the charts when it comes to measuring passion and pleasure. In effect, judging a partner by these standards acts as an insurance policy against repeating your parents' mistakes. Unfortunately, this puts a lot of pressure on you and your partner, and sets you both up for expectations that might be unrealistic.

Look back over your past relationships and understand the patterns. Have you had a series of short-term affairs? When the lust wore off, did you worry that you had made the wrong choice and started looking for the right person all over again? If this is the case, talk to your current partner about your feelings, rather than going cold and distant, and look for solutions to your fears and anxieties. Understanding the reality that lust is not built to last, but instead functions as a preparation to endure to the next stage, the bonding stage, may prevent you from ditching your current partner before you get a chance to work on the relationship. There is another potential upside: overcoming these worries could bring you closer to each other.

## BONDING: Six Months to Three Years

By this stage in your relationship, you can officially call each other boyfriend and girlfriend, but you are still getting to know each other and deciding if this relationship is for keeps. Part of the process is making certain your sexual tastes are compatible.

Rather than telling your partner what you don't like, which will probably make him or her defensive or withdrawn, focus on what you do enjoy and try building on that. Start by talking about an occasion or a time when things went well and then look at what you can learn from that experience and how to incorporate those lessons into your love-making today.

## SETTLED: Three+ Years

When you were dating, your relationship was based on doing enjoyable things together. However, now you have moved in together, and there is danger of your relationship becoming centered on running a house and paying the bills rather than having fun.

Shake up your lovemaking by surrendering to the creativity of play— tease each other, chase each other around the house, or get messy together. Use the whole house and not just the bedroom. Life and sex do not always have to be serious and "grown up." Allow your inner child to emerge, access her or his imagination, and return to a time before you started censoring yourself.

## Parenting

Babies and small children have the ability to destroy everything they touch: your furniture, your nerves, and most important, your sex life.

Make your bedroom a loving refuge and put a lock on the door. (If there is an emergency, your children can knock.) This will not only allow you to make love without the fear of being interrupted but teach your children an important lesson for when they grow up: parents should never forget they are lovers too.

There is more practical advice on how to flirt and keep romance alive—even though you have children—in my book *I Love You but You Always Put Me Last: Why the Kids-First Approach to Parenting Is Hurting Your Marriage—and the Proven Plan to Restore Balance*.

## Personal Reinvention

If your partner is going through a midlife crisis or a life-altering event like the loss of a job or a parent's death and he or she is beginning to question everything—especially your sex life—it is easy to become frightened and panic.

Instead of being defensive and "talking up" your joint sex life, use your partner's honesty about his or her unhappiness to look at your own feelings about sex, what it means to you, and how your joint lovemaking can be improved. Next, imagine for a second that every word your partner is saying is true—at least from where he or she is standing. Ask plenty of questions and check out that you've heard his or her message correctly. Finally, start negotiating both your visions for a reinvented sex life and what experiments you'd like to try. In this way, you can be an ally in your partner's journey of discovery rather than an enemy.

## Glory Days

When your children are older, there is more time to relax, spend quality time with your partner, and get on the same sexual wavelength.

Although your current comfort zone feels safe, too much safety can kill desire. So take a small risk and test if your fears are correct. Will your partner really be so shocked? You might be turned down, and that's unpleasant, but could you handle a small amount of rejection, especially as you've only taken a small risk? Ultimately, nothing is worse than the helplessness of just lying back and accepting the status quo.

## EXERCISE 2   KNOW THE RULES FOR TALKING ABOUT SEX

The better you know someone, the easier it should be to talk about sex. Unfortunately, the opposite is likelier to be true. Time and again, I find couples are left guessing what each other likes and doesn't like, often making false assumptions. So how do you talk about this most sensitive of subjects?

1. **Never talk about sex in the bedroom.** Although your bedroom is a private space, it is too loaded for such an intimate discussion. If the conversation happens after sex, one partner can easily take it as a bad review. If the conversation happens as you're getting undressed, one partner can take it as an invitation to make love. Better scenarios for talking are long car journeys (it's hard for one person to storm off) or over dinner (eating can cover potentially embarrassing silences or provide thinking time). I've also had clients who've discussed sex in a shared bath—a sensual rather than purely sexual space.

2. **Concentrate on the positive.** Most people have insecurities about sex. We worry about our bodies, our technique, and lack of knowledge. So even the most innocuous statements can be heard as criticism. Therefore, "I need to talk about our sex life" is often heard as "You're crappy in bed," or "I think we need to spice things up" is interpreted as "I'm going to cheat on you." To get around these problems, start with a positive statement: "I really enjoy our lovemaking," or "I was thinking about that wonderful time when we . . ." Follow up with a question that invites your partner to think creatively: "How can we build on that?" If you have any complaints, frame them in a positive way. Instead of "You're too rough," phrase it as "I like it when you really take your time." Instead of "You never seem to relax," try "I get turned on when I know you're really enjoying yourself."

3. **Avoid using words that raise the stakes.** As soon as you say "never"

or "always," your partner will get defensive or remember the exception to the rule and start a fight over it. Own the statement "I feel" instead of "You make me feel."

4. **Be as specific as possible.** When my clients first talk about sex, they always use such generalities that I have no idea what they mean. So try to be as precise as possible. Instead of saying, "I'd like longer cuddles," give an indication: "I'd like us to cuddle for at least five minutes"; otherwise, your partner might be thinking you're asking for hours of foreplay. Instead of "I wish you'd make more of an effort," which could mean anything, ask for what you really want: "Can you wear that lingerie I bought you?"

5. **Show rather than tell.** When communicating during lovemaking, a touch is worth a thousand words. So take your partner's hand and put it where you'd like to be caressed, and guide his or her hand by pushing it down (for firmer touch) or raising it slightly (for gentler touch). If things go wrong, never turn your back in a huff (this will be interpreted as rejection).

## EXERCISE 3    LEXICON FOR LOVEMAKING

One of the biggest barriers to talking about sex is that we don't have a working vocabulary to refer to parts of the body and the various types of lovemaking. So in the first counseling sessions (where there is a sexual focus), I go out of my way to name as many "forbidden" words as possible, partly to normalize them but mainly to remove any embarrassment.

Sometimes to break the ice, I get couples to come up with as many names as possible for the male and female sexual organs (even the slang ones). Personally, I use the medical terms whenever possible:

| | | | |
|---|---|---|---|
| Vagina | Foreskin | Anus | Breasts |
| Penis | Testicles | Buttocks | Nipples |

**Masturbate:** to pleasure yourself or your partner using your fingers and hand or with sex toys

**Oral Sex:** to pleasure your partner using your tongue, lips, and mouth

**Intercourse:** penetrating the vagina with the penis

**Erection:** when a man's penis is stiff and ready to penetrate

**Flaccid:** when a man's penis is in its normal unaroused state

**Lubricated:** when a woman's vagina is aroused and ready to be penetrated

**Orgasm:** a pleasurable involuntary reflex action

**Semen:** thick whitish fluid produced in a man's testicles

**Ejaculate:** the release of semen when a man climaxes

**Premature Ejaculation:** a lack of control over ejaculation

**Retarded Ejaculation:** an inability to ejaculate by intercourse however long it continues

**Erectile Dysfunction:** the inability to maintain an erection long enough to have intercourse

**Anorgasmia:** the inability to orgasm

**Vaginismus:** a condition where a woman's vagina cannot be penetrated

Practice saying these words and terms, first to yourself, and then out loud. It may be embarrassing at first. After all, you've had years of practice skirting them. Keep in mind that your partner may also be as shy about using them as you. However, the more you say them, the less awkward they will sound.

# Chapter Two

# Your Relationship Outside the Bedroom

Whether your love life is good and you're looking to make it even better or poor and seeking to improve it, sex must be put in the context of the rest of your relationship. If there are unresolved issues or one of you feels taken for granted, the general unhappiness will slowly seep into the bedroom, and however good your technique or overall sexual compatibility, the passion will drain from your lovemaking. This is why I always ask couples coming into counseling about sex, even if they seek my help for other reasons, because boredom and dissatisfaction are key indicators of buried conflict or avoidance of pressing problems.

When your love life is routine or infrequent, it is easy to blame outside factors: "We're so busy," "It's the children," "We never seem to go to bed at the same time," or "All marriages go through bad patches." Few couples want to look much deeper and either resign themselves to "okay" sex or resolve to try harder. Accepting okay sex can take the pressure off and stop couples from blaming each other. Trying harder will sometimes improve lovemaking for a while, but before long, everything settles back into the same patterns. So what's really going on?

Glenda and Graham were in their late forties. He had a successful accounting firm, where Glenda worked as office manager, and their daughter had recently left home. Financially secure and with no significant responsibilities, it should have been a great phase of their lives, but they were both unhappy. "I feel like a spectator in my own life," explained Glenda. "All these things are happening, but I'm not really involved."

Graham was equally puzzled. "I always thought that once our daughter was off our hands, we would start putting each other first, but somehow it doesn't seem to happen. We're always doing things for other people."

Their sex life had ground to a halt, partly because Glenda had a hysterectomy three years previously and partly because neither felt comfortable having sex when their daughter was in the house. "I just can't relax," explained Glenda. If Glenda's health and their daughter had been the real reasons why they made love only two or three times a year, they should have already made significant progress. Instead, they felt despondent and stuck.

So I looked at their general communication.

"I feel Graham undermines me. He's always telling me what to do," explained Glenda.

Naturally, Graham saw things differently. "I only want what's best for you."

Glenda countered this with an example. "I have never been a very confident driver, and I started driving less and less, letting Graham do the lion's share. However, I told myself *this has got to stop,* and so I took advanced lessons and passed. On our first trip out together, he told me, 'Look out for that car pulling out from the left,' and that was it. I've not driven since."

It soon became clear that Graham's interventions were meant to be helpful, but because he found it difficult to express his emotions, he would behave detached, cautious, and aware of every risk. For Graham and Glenda to be intimate in the bedroom, I needed to help them dismantle the barriers they had erected to protect themselves in their day-to-day lives before they could work on their sexual problems.

In my experience, couples who are dissatisfied with their love lives fit into one of five patterns:

1. *Friends rather than lovers*

2. *Separate tracks*

3. *Mismatched levels of desire*

4. *Polarized ideas of expressing love*

5. *Expecting too much from our partner*

## Friends Rather Than lovers

The modern trend is for our partner to be our best friend too and there-fore supportive, endlessly understanding, and prepared to accept us as we are. That's all fine in theory, but being best friends makes it harder for a couple to argue because friends don't have blazing arguments. In the meantime, longer working hours and fewer social outings mean that most of us have a smaller circle of friends and see them less often. These changes have reinforced the central importance of our partner, and with all our emotional eggs in one basket, it is doubly difficult for us to argue. However, it is impossible for two people to live in close proximity without conflict, but to "agree to disagree" or suppress their annoyance, irritation, or anger for the sake of keeping the peace is a dangerous trap. Because anger and passion are inextricably linked, the "peace" might result in fewer arguments, but there isn't much lovemaking either.

Unfortunately, we can't pick and choose which feelings we push down and which we express. Often we end up repressing all our feelings —including the ones we want like passion and joy and ones we might need. Graham and Glenda certainly fit this category: instead of letting their anger rise to the surface and creating the sense that "some-thing must be done," they had settled into a superficially friendly rela-tionship that swept the issues under the surface and was largely devoid of sexual passion.

### *The Crux*

When we stop seeing our partners as separate from us, we desexualize them. Instead of being a sensual and sexual human being, they are exten-sions of us, which removes the individuality about the person that once drew us. Desire needs space as well as closeness, so make certain there is time for both of you to pursue separate hobbies and interests. I often rec-ommend clients to witness each other in their own environments. For example, picking him up for lunch (and seeing the respect in his col-leagues' eyes) or watching her give a conference speech (and listening to the applause) helps people become aware of how interesting, respected, and capable the other is.

*"Desire needs space as well as closeness."*

## Separate Tracks

While some couples are too close and turn into roommates, others are too far apart and become strangers. These partners are on parallel train tracks, aware of each other's movements, waving as they pass in the kitchen but seldom getting really close. In my experience, there are normally three different scenarios that prompt separate tracks relationships.

First are couples with fundamental differences that cannot be reconciled. For example, Matt, thirty-nine, and Karen, thirty-six, had been in an on-off relationship for ten years.

"When I look back, I wonder if we're right for each other," said Karen in their first joint session. "I want to settle down and have children, but Matt has never been ready."

Over their time together, the closest they had come to living together was Matt renting an apartment around the corner from Karen.

"But I did spend most of my time at your place," said Matt.

"Except you never had your mail sent to my place, and if we had a fight, you'd disappear back to your place."

The couple had split and come back together several times.

"I think I've seen the last of him, and I'll start seeing someone else, but he'll pop up again all sad and missing me," said Karen. "We'll have a coffee and agree to try again, but nothing really changes."

"Is it like you can't live with and you can't live without each other either?" I asked.

They nodded. Their sex life had been good during the lust stage, the memory of which was what was keeping them together, but Karen could never really relax and enjoy their lovemaking as she was always expecting him to leave. In effect, they were truly on separate tracks as neither their day-to-day lives nor their futures were intertwined.

In the second kind of separate tracks relationships, the couple does bond and forms a lasting relationship, but children, career, or circumstances set them on different courses. James and Marie, the "glory days" couple, are a good example of this scenario.

"I always put my career first. In fact, I was so selfish that when Marie's father was dying and she was nursing him around the clock, I still went away on business," admitted James. "There was nobody to look after the children, and in the end, my sister picked up the slack."

"Why didn't you ask him to stay?" I asked Marie.

"I thought it was obvious that I needed him . . . we needed him, but I didn't want to beg. In fact, I covered up for him, telling everybody that he was closing a big deal when all along I knew he was just attending a quarterly board meeting."

"It sounds like you were frightened to ask in case he said no," I said.

"What sort of marriage is that?" Marie wondered aloud.

Their sex life had been perfunctory, neither taking a risk outside the bedroom to tackle their real issues.

While the second type of separate tracks couple ignores important issues, the third kind puts them under the spotlight. Unfortunately, although these couples argue a lot, they never find a resolution. At the beginning, high-conflict relationships can produce fireworks in the bedroom, especially when the couple is making up after a fight. However, after a while, the arguments spill over into their sex life.

"We were having sex, but she was just lying there," said Jake, forty-two.

"I was tired," replied his partner, Chloe, twenty-eight.

"So, I thought, *Why am I bothering?* and stopped."

"And we argued about it the whole weekend."

"Exactly," Jake said turning away. "What's the point?"

Although their sex life had taken the brunt, there were fundamental issues driving the anger that weren't being addressed. Chloe wanted children, but Jake had had one family and didn't want another. Until these topics could be talked about sensibly, they were doomed to remain on separate tracks.

### The Crux

Sex oftentimes is a symptom, not the disease. When you strip away the distractions and coping mechanisms, what is your relationship really like? What fundamental issues are not being discussed?

Commit to going through the next few weeks with your eyes wide open, truly mindful of the patterns in your relationship. Put bruised ego aside and scheme up something to bring the two of you together. It doesn't matter how extravagant—a weekend getaway or popcorn and a favorite movie. The point is to relax a bit and to foster an environment that promotes calm and effective communication.

## Mismatched Levels of Desire

It is easy for one partner to take all the "blame" for a sexual problem or for a couple to blame each other. For example, Mike and Jenny, whose sex life had dwindled since the birth of their daughter and a subsequent miscarriage, alternated between labeling themselves and each other as the cause of their unhappiness.

"If I'm not in the mood, he gets huffy," said Jenny. "He asks time after time until I'm worn down and say, 'Just get it over with.' Anything to keep the peace."

Unfortunately, Mike felt pestering was his only way of getting sex. "I have to keep asking because I'll eventually get lucky."

When Jenny wasn't angry with Mike, she was angry with herself, admitting, "I wish I could be a normal wife and mother and enjoy sex."

Although the blame game was rampant, I believed the problem was in the way Mike and Jenny communicated about sex, as well as how they negotiated about the frequency of sex. Communication is not up to one partner or the other, it is a joint responsibility. What's more, by reframing the problem as different levels of desire, rather than anyone's fault, it becomes a *shared* problem.

> *"It is very easy for one partner to take all the 'blame'*
> *for a sexual problem or for a couple to blame each other."*

In my experience, blame makes people defensive and unable to see the bigger picture. Once blame has been taken out of the equation, a couple can start working like a team, and the differences in their levels of desire become much more manageable.

## The Crux

Try this quick quiz with your partner. Don't think about the answers too much; just write the first thing down that comes to mind.

1. When I think of love, I think of . . .

2. When I think of sex, I think of . . .

3. In a typical month, how often would you like to have sex?

4. In a typical month, how often do you think your partner would like to have sex?

When I gave this quiz to Mike and Jenny, they came up with similar answers to questions one and two. Interestingly, they both wanted to have sex *eight* times a month. However, Jenny thought Mike wanted sex "every day," and he thought she wanted sex "never." They were surprised and delighted to discover their idea of the other's level of desire was a long way from reality.

## Polarized Ideas of Expressing Love

The highest form of intimacy rated by many people comes in verbal communication. We want access to our partners' private thoughts and consider talking essential in learning their feelings. No wonder we are forever asking, "What are you thinking?" and "Penny for your thoughts." If somehow our partners do not match our level of self-disclosure or openness, we feel cheated and angry.

Julie and Ian, both in their early thirties, started counseling after an argument turned nasty and Ian disappeared for twenty-four hours. "I don't know how to start getting Ian to open up to me and have constructive communication. He cannot see anything we need to discuss. Still, he couldn't be a nicer person. Believe it or not, he has always bent over backward for me."

I suspected that Ian communicated his feelings in a different way than Julie, especially as male identity has generally been based on self-control and hiding weakness. So I explained the five languages of love and intimacy: appreciative words, caring actions, gift giving, creating quality time, and affectionate physical contact. It was clear that Julie used appreciative words, but just because that was *her* love language, it was unfair for her to expect her husband to be fluent as well.

"He's an intelligent man but really can't see what troubles me and seems a bit thick emotionally," said Julie.

So I got her to look at whether she had been so focused on him speaking her language that she had not heard him communicating in his own.

The next week, Julie returned with a smile. "You were spot on about our different ways of showing love. Neither 'languages' are wrong, but we need to respect each other's way of communicating. Previously, when he did stuff for me, I just thought he was practical, not that he was showing his feelings for me. So I told him how thoughtful he was for doing the shopping for me when he was on the way home from his mother's house. He couldn't wait to show me what he had bought. I picked up on it. I think it seems he's really saying, 'I did this for you.' I could also see he was relieved that I appreciated him."

Although I don't like to make generalizations about men and women, it is true that many men feel more comfortable using affectionate physical contact than affectionate words. So I am always saddened when women say, "He's only interested in one thing." Their partner is probably asking to be close the only way he knows how.

> *"It is true that many men feel more comfortable using affectionate physical contact than affectionate words."*

### The Crux

If you have always focused on talking, consider the other side of the coin: listening. Next time your partner tells you something, monitor yourself. Are you giving him or her your full attention? (Don't take a sneak peak at your phone or turn away to make dinner; make and keep good eye contact.) Whenever you're tempted to interrupt, even when your partner is rambling or having trouble expressing him- or herself, bite the inside of your cheek. (Your partner may simply need time to warm up before moving on to something meaningful.) In fact, the very act of talking to you should not be taken for granted, even if it's not "meaningful" or of interest to you. Encourage your partner by participating in "active listening," nodding from time to time and repeating back the last sentence he or she said, e.g., "So you hailed a taxi?" (This proves to your partner that you're truly engaged.)

## RELATIONSHIP PARADOXES

Some of the skills that make for a good relationship outside the bedroom can destroy passion inside. To bring a fresh perspective, I have outlined three common ideas about how you and your partner should relate to each other, which on the surface seem great but have an unexpected downside too. Look through the list and decide if any of them are undermining your sex life.

1. *Intimacy is about being valued and accepted, thereby prompting a warm, cozy atmosphere where love can thrive.* Except, this is only part of the story. Real intimacy involves sharing the difficult bits of ourselves too, which are possibly less acceptable to our partner than hiding them. Unfortunately, many couples are fixated on safety and security. This is fine but also promotes polite rather than passionate or exciting lovemaking.

2. *Relationships are all about compromise.* Certainly compromise helps in arguments or when deciding how to spend spare time. (For example, he will play golf on Saturday but get back in time for a family lunch.) However, in the bedroom, too much compromise can be a disaster. It provides an unappealing tit-for-tat situation in which each partner will "give in to," instead of enjoy (not particularly satisfying for anyone).

3. *A good partner should make us feel valued and acceptable.* This means we get angry and resentful if our partner cannot pull off this difficult trick. But, ultimately, we need to be able to validate ourselves too. In fact, the paradox here is that when we don't validate ourselves, our partner will find it difficult or impossible to do as well.

## Expecting Too Much from Your Partner

In successful and happy relationships, each partner looks after each other. Traditionally, this has included the more practical elements like earning enough money to provide for material needs, or cooking, cleaning, and running a house. More recently, this has expanded to looking out for each other's emotional needs. Unfortunately, in some couples, the expectations have grown even greater—to surpass being supportive and cheering them on to being responsible for their well-being. With this new mindset, if you're suffering from low self-esteem or are angry or unhappy, you might think it is because your partner has not been supportive enough, has behaved badly, or does not properly understand your needs. In the bedroom, if you're not turned on, it is because he or she is not pushing the right buttons or making you feel desired enough.

Emily, thirty-one, has been married for a little over a year but had known her husband for several years before. "Our sex life has never been passionate, but I don't think I noticed (or tried to ignore it) as he often works away, so I blamed it on that. However, sex has always been an important part of my previous relationships, and I am now feeling unattractive and miss being desired."

Instead of wondering how she could feel more attractive and desired herself, Emily had passed this responsibility on to her husband. "He says he does find me attractive, but is quite childish in the ways he shows it by quickly groping me in an almost comical teenage-boy type of way."

### The Crux

Take a fresh look at problems both inside and outside the bedroom. First, ask yourself, *How can I communicate my needs differently and make it easier for my partner to take them on board?* Next, ask, *Am I expecting too much?* Especially when you are dealing with long-term health problems (your own or your children's), a bereavement, or other stressful event, it is easy to be overwhelmed and make demands that your partner is not equipped to fulfill.

## SOMETHING TO SLEEP ON

**In summary, remember:**

- Good relationships need balance. If a couple gets too close and/or never argue, each partner's individual identity can get swallowed up into a bland couple sexuality (based on what each person doesn't mind rather than what they truly want).

- Conversely, if a couple is too separate, there is never enough trust to be truly intimate or for anything beyond fleeting moments of "make-up" sex.

# SEX ED

### EXERCISE 4    DISCLOSURE

Knowing your partner's sexual history can help you determine if there are any past events still casting a shadow today. It is hard, however, to cover this topic without the possibility of breeding jealousy or insecurity, which is why I recommend sharing the story of your introduction to the birds and the bees because it often feels safe but is also revealing. For instance, here is what Graham, forty-seven, had to say about his first lessons in human sexuality.

Toward the end of the Easter term in seventh grade at my all-boys school, a rumor went around that we were going to cover sex in biology. I must have been about twelve, and I'd already gleaned a basic understanding by noticing our pet guinea pigs on the lawn. I'd read the relevant section in my biology book, with its cross-sectional diagrams of male and female sexual organs, but most of my knowledge came from classmates. For example, I'd been told that Henry VIII had caught syphilis from too much masturbation and that men had erections to prevent them from urinating into women's vaginas! So when our biology teacher Mr. Osbourne finally confirmed that our next lesson was on sex, there was a buzz of anticipation.

When the lesson finally arrived, it was a huge letdown. Mr. Osbourne went into great detail about how single-cell creatures reproduce by splitting in two. There was also a lesson on how worms were hermaphrodites. It was not until halfway through lesson three that we graduated on to humans. There was a very biological explanation of how eggs were released from the fallopian tubes, the competition between sperm to fertilize an egg, and the length of the human gestation period. There was nothing about pleasure, emotions, or relationships. When a red-faced Mr. Osbourne got through the lesson, he tentatively asked if we had any questions. We had millions, but nobody dared put their hand up. When the bell rang, it was hard to know who was most relieved—him or us.

Graham's story is comprehensive and detailed, and I encourage you and your partner to share in the same way. What other sources of information did you have to learn about sex? (Books, TV, pornography?) How accurate? How informative? What messages did you receive about sex? What influence did these formative lessons have? What is the impact on your love life today?

Discuss what you've learned about each other and what you've realized about yourself from your story. Is there anything that you would like to change about your lovemaking or your perceptions of lovemaking?

For example, Graham realized that his introduction to sex had been cold, clinical, and intellectual. So he discussed with his partner, Glenda, how to bring more emotion into the bedroom. Their prescription was to look at each other more and to stop or slow down for hugs and kisses.

## EXERCISE 5    MESSAGES ABOUT MASCULINITY AND FEMININITY

One of the constant themes of this book is the need for couples to talk more. Here is a set of prompts that I sometimes use in therapy to understand the messages that we have been given by our parents, friends, the media, and the wider society. Try discussing them with your partner and discover what promotes and what hinders good sex.

*What positive messages are there about men?*

*What negative messages are there about men?*

*What positive messages are there about women?*

*What negative messages are there about women?*

*How I hope this book will change my mind about men and sex.*

*How I hope this book will change my mind about women and sex.*

*What I believed at eighteen about men and women.*

*What I believe today.*

*What I would like to believe.*

## EXERCISE 6    WHAT'S REALLY ON YOUR MIND

Most couples find it hard to communicate what they're really thinking because they love each other and don't want to cause upset or be critical. So they bite their tongues, smile, and move on. Unfortunately, there is only so long you can hold back before you explode a mess of issues, which is so overwhelming to your partner that he or she will shut down, get defensive, or make a counterattack. This exercise not only helps you avoid this under-sharing/oversharing trap, it provides a safe framework in which to discuss difficult issues.

✓ Flip a coin to decide who goes first. The winner has three minutes to explain what's really on his or her mind. (For example, it could be something arising from the disclosure exercise.)

✓ Set the alarm on your phone or use an egg timer.

✓ Meanwhile, the other person will listen—without interrupting until the time is up.

✓ When the alarm goes off, even if the person talking is in mid-sentence, he or she must stop.

✓ The person listening does not respond to what has been said (that opportunity will come later), but must summarize what's been said.

✓ Afterward, the speaker should confirm that the summary is correct or make a correction to anything wrong. For example, "I said I *think* it's wrong, not that *it is* wrong." He or she can also add anything important that has been missed from their partner's summary.

✓ Now it is the turn of the listener to become the talker and have his or her three minutes while the other person listens and offers a summation.

✓ Repeat this process two or three times or until you have both covered what's on your mind.

✓ Afterward, discuss what you've learned about your partner, what problems you identified, and what changes each of you can make to resolve the situation.

# Chapter Three

# The Road to Repair

Gordon, thirty-two, and Maya, twenty-eight, are thoughtful and considerate. Gordon always thinks before he speaks in case he says something hurtful. Maya looks up to Gordon and values his opinions about her art (she is a part-time potter) and his knowledge of marketing and networking, which has gotten her work into several group exhibitions. On the face of things, they are the perfect couple: empathetic, involved in each other's dreams and ambitions, and mutually interdependent. Unfortunately, their sex life is a disaster.

"We make love about once a month," explained Gordon.

"If that," Maya chipped in, "and I'm always the one to make the first move."

"I'll give Maya her due; she's always very encouraging. She'll dance in an erotic way or put on sexy underwear, but I'm not often in the mood." He smiled and shrugged his shoulders.

"How does that make you feel?" I asked Maya.

"He has very high standards. All his girlfriends have been gorgeous."

"I've never been unfaithful or ever given you reason to doubt me," Gordon replied.

I sensed there was something more and encouraged him to continue.

"But I don't want to hurt Maya."

She had already reached for the tissues. "I have some idea of what he's going to say."

"What good is it going to do?" he asked me.

It was obvious that Gordon was about to explain why he seldom felt desire for Maya. While it was admirable that he had kept back hurtful information, it had still leaked out, probably in hints, jokes, or exasperated putdowns immediately taken back. Maya had already been hurt. Her sexual confidence was low, and being repeatedly knocked down had undermined her self-esteem. Indeed, the more we talked about sex, even in a general way, the more often she reached for the tissues. Not surprisingly, Gordon became more and more reticent. However, until his issues were directly voiced, Maya could not challenge him, which left them both unable to find a way to deal with their problems.

So what did Gordon need to say?

"There are certain odors that I don't like," he confessed.

When it comes to dealing with sex, it is important to call a spade a spade, so slowly I encouraged him to be more direct.

"Maya likes to be spontaneous about sex, but if she hasn't had a shower for several hours, I don't like the smell of her vagina."

"I know that unless we've just got out of the shower, sex is not going to happen," said Maya.

The whole atmosphere in the room had completely changed. Maya had imagined something far worse, so now she had a chance to tell her side and we could work on improving their love life.

So what if the problem is that you love your partner but something about him or her is turning you off? It's a surprisingly common problem and one that couples find really hard to resolve. So what's the best way forward? A white lie? Sure, nobody gets hurt but sex remains infrequent and unsatisfactory. Or tell the truth and risk damaging the relationship forever?

Before you start confessing your issues to each other, it is important to ask yourself two fundamental questions:

1. *Can my partner do something about this complaint?* If your partner's behavior is upsetting and interfering with your sex life, it is important to be honest and explain. Gordon's complaint about smell is fine because it is something that Maya could easily change. Other examples of acceptable complaints include "making more of an effort and wearing stylish clothes when we go out as this puts me into the mood

for lovemaking when we return" or "please cut your fingernails because the jagged edges hurt me." However, I had to stop Gordon from making remarks about Maya's weight as that was not something she could easily remedy, and, anyway, it feeds directly into the second question.

2. *Are my criticisms fair?* All too often, we are criticizing something that our partner cannot change. For example, Gordon had put the blame for his decreasing desire on "neither of us getting any younger or more attractive," and although he tried to include himself, Maya was despondent. "I can't stop time." There is another way in which a criticism is unfair. Sometimes when we dislike something about ourselves, instead of accepting our frailties or trying to change them, we distance ourselves by focusing on our partner and complaining about the very same behavior or fault we have. (This is called "projecting" feelings onto someone else.) So, for example, Gordon admitted later in counseling that he had deep anxieties about aging himself and had lots of negative feelings about his thickening waist and thinning hairline.

If you have answered yes to the two questions above, discuss your issues with your partner. However, remember to be *specific* (or your partner will imagine far worse) and to *own* the problems (or your partner will hear only criticism). For example say, "When you wear your winter nightie, I find it hard to get aroused" instead of "You turn me off." If you answered no to either question, please keep your issues to yourself for the time being. It is unfair to dump on your partner or to dramatically undermine his or her self-esteem (and it is counterproductive to better lovemaking).

## PREPARING YOURSELF FOR A RICHER LOVE LIFE

Through my research I was saddened to learn that many people had low expectations of the likelihood of improving their love life. When asked "Do you think you can change your sex life?" 35 percent of respondents to my online survey reported they were not completely confident and 14 percent had no confidence at all. Unfortunately, we believe that we have to transform ourselves (by becoming slimmer, sexier, and more skilled) or our circumstances (by finding more time or hiring babysitters more often). No wonder we feel trapped and dispirited. My message, however, is that great sex is not reserved for the young, good looking, and knowledgeable. It is for everybody, and the best news of all is the ingredients to great sex are locked inside each and every one of us. So what are these magic factors?

The answer will probably come as a shock, because when I asked people what would improve their love life, they gave all the predictable answers:

- Feeling closer to my partner—52 percent

- Better communication—53 percent

- More time—38 percent

However, the two qualities guaranteed to revolutionize your love life are actually none of these usual suspects. What really spices things up, no matter the issue or the stage of your relationship, are imagination and confidence.

## Imagination

If you lived in a fairy tale and could have just one wish to improve your sex life, the best choice would be to have a good imagination. I rate imagination as even more critical than confidence because unless you can dream it, you can't do it. There are also helpful cousins of imagination like creativity (vital for keeping passion alive) and the ability to find a way around fears and inhibitions (and there will be plenty of those on the journey ahead).

If your heart sunk when I stressed the importance of imagination, you are not alone. When I go into businesses and charities with my writer's hat on to teach staff how to unlock imagination, I can smell the worry and fear in the room: "I was hopeless at stories at school," "It's not for me," "I can't spell," "People will laugh."

It is entirely different when I go into elementary schools and encourage children to be creative and improve their writing skills. I take a large box filled with strange items and the pupils have to go up one by one and take something out. Afterward, we go around the room and each child tells a story based on the object they chose. In their imagination, a hollow bone that my dog has chewed becomes a telescope to see into the future, an orange squeezer is a spaceship, and a key unlocks buried pirate treasure. However, once the pupils have reached high school, a bone is just a bone, an orange squeezer is for making juice, and the key opens a front door. Although they tell great stories, these teenagers have lost the ability to escape into different worlds.

Something about going through puberty makes us stunted in the real world, which is ironic when you consider how much we need that childish sense of wonder to keep our passion alive. So how can you turn back the clock and undo the damage done by a school system focused on exams and corporations focused on hitting the bottom line?

*"Something about going through puberty makes us stunted in the real world, which is ironic when you consider how much we need that childish sense of wonder to keep our passion alive."*

Think of your imagination like a muscle that has gone flabby; with a little training, it will soon become a flexible and powerful asset to improving your sex life. Here are three ways of giving your imagination a workout.

1. *Be more aware of your senses.* Modern life is so hectic that we seldom stop and stare. And if we fail to notice anything during the daytime, what chance is there of being fully conscious in our dreams? Go somewhere that you won't be interrupted and either sit or lie down. Take ten minutes out of your day and one by one focus on the following senses:

   - *Look.* Soak in all the sights around you. Become aware of the varied shapes and patterns—the angle of a park bench, the wrapper on a bar of chocolate, the color of the flowers, or the pigeon perched on the back of a park bench.

- *Listen.* Tune in to the different sounds. Start with the loudest ones, perhaps the echo of footsteps in an atrium. What is the pitch? What is the cadence? How does the cadence change? What are the other sounds mixing in? Perhaps traffic outside, birds, or conversations? How do they echo around the space? What about the silence? Is that layered too? Can you hear wind through the trees or the hum of a soda machine in a hallway?

- *Touch.* Feel the texture of the grass beneath you and not just with your fingers but the back of your hand or your forearm. Take off your shoes and enjoy the warmth (or the coolness) of the earth under your toes. Pick up something and feel its weight in your hand.

- *Smell.* We're generally only aware of the strongest smell, but with a little time and practice, you'll begin to distinguish the layers here too. Close your eyes, so you can really immerse yourself. Can you smell the earth, freshly cut grass, concrete dust from a nearby building site, or maybe the almond croissant of the person at the next table?

- *Taste.* Run the tip of your tongue over your lips. How do they taste? Let your tongue roam over your teeth; get the saliva going. Can you find the aftertaste of your last meal? The minty taste from your morning brushing?

- *Emotions.* What are you feeling? Joy, happiness, emptiness, regret? How many different emotions can you identify? How do your feelings overlap?

- *Be aware of your awareness.* You don't have to live your life with your senses switched off. Find beauty where you least expect it—the shade of yellow on your neighbor's porch. Hear the music and rhythm beneath the clatter and hum of the nearby building site. Enjoy the texture of the spikey potted plant in your office foyer. Once fully conscious of these small wonders, you'll be more prepared for being sensual in the bedroom rather than expecting to go from zero to sixty when your partner makes his or her first move.

2. *Explore your dreams.* Have you ever been in the middle of a dream and something bizarre happened, like you can fly or you've been intro-

duced to the president in your dressing gown, and you've suddenly realized *Hang on, I must be dreaming?* You are doing something that Dutch psychiatrist Fredrik van Eeden (1860–1932) called "lucid dreaming," which is defined as being aware that you are in a dream rather than in reality. So how can you harness this power to boost your imagination?

- *Get more rest.* The longer that you're asleep, the longer and closer together the dreams will be. While the first dream of the night is only ten minutes long, after eight hours your dreams last between forty-five minutes and an hour.

- *Prime yourself to dream.* As you're lying in bed about to drift off to sleep, tell yourself, *I'm going to dream tonight, and I'm going to remember it.* Repeat this instruction a couple of times.

- *Look out for the signs that you're dreaming.* The classic signals of a dream include: you're doing something strange (breathing under water), items in this world are strange (dogs talk or pavements move), other people are acting strangely (they have tentacles rather than arms), or you're in a strange context (you're Madonna's lover or talking to someone who is dead).

- *Tell yourself, "I'm dreaming."* Being aware that you are in the middle of a dream takes away anxiety and allows you to explore this other world.

- *When you wake up, stay still.* Moving makes the dream harder to remember. In contrast, if you keep still, various fragments will return. Ask yourself, *What was I doing in my dream when I woke up? What was I thinking? What did I feel?* Recall the context and assemble all the clues about what happened. Then ask what happened before that and track backward. By reliving the dream in reverse, you'll remember more.

3. *Write down your dreams.* Keep a piece of paper and a pen by the bed and record what happened immediately after you wake up.

- *Scribbled notes are enough.* You do not have to write an essay, just a few words and prompts.

- *Describe the images and characters.* Just get a few vivid fragments down, rather than trying to explain the strange logic of the dream world or attempting to make sense of it.

- *Imagine you can move around in this world.* Taking the moments of a recovered dream, what happens if you move the story forward or backward? What would happen if, for example, you went outside or pulled back a curtain? How do you feel? Write down all your discoveries.

## THE HEALING POWER OF LUCID DREAMS

Research at Stanford University has revealed that lucid dreaming occurs during the highly activated phase of REM (rapid eye movement) sleep when there is also increased vaginal blood flow or erections. This explains why there is a sexual component to so many dreams. Further:

- *Lucid dreaming is a pleasure in its own right.* By valuing your dreams, you consider yourself worthy of a little indulgence instead of someone who has a lot to get done.

- *Lucid dreaming makes you feel good.* My clients report being carried through the morning on a wave of bliss.

- *Lucid dreaming helps you look freshly at the world.* One client told me that as she dressed that morning, the sun shone through the blinds, casting patterns across the duvet that looked like a giant barcode.

- *Lucid dreaming provides fresh material for your fantasies.* All too often, we use secondhand stimulation from movies or pornography. These might be effective in the same way that fast food fills us up, but ultimately, a home-cooked meal tastes better and properly sustains us. A lucid dream is fuel for your imagination.

- *Lucid dreaming helps make you a more sensual person.* In this way, you will have a richer palette to bring to your lovemaking.

- *The act of writing helps dream recall.* Instead of the dream slipping away, it will stay with you. (In Chapter Seven, we will look at how dreams can feed fantasies, and you might find it helpful to refer back to previous lucid dreams.)

## Confidence

In my survey, 100 percent of women and 20 percent of men thought their love lives would improve if they had better bodies. Unfortunately, many people, like Jenny, whom we met earlier, don't just stop at wanting to be slimmer or have better muscle tone, they actively hate their bodies. "I didn't really like it before I had my daughter but now . . ."

"I think you've got a lovely body," Mike reassured Jenny.

"You don't have to look at it, well, you do, but not as often as I do," replied Jenny. "I'll be drying myself after a bath and catch myself in the mirror and shudder. Even when I'm dressed and my scar from my C-section is not on display, I still know it's there."

It was not surprising that Jenny found it hard to relax and enjoy love-making (and preferred to keep the light off).

Over the past twenty-five years, I have seen an increasing number of people with poor body image. Perhaps it is not surprising that our sense of a "normal" body has been distorted so dramatically, particularly for women, thanks to pornography, magazines, clothing sizes, and celebrities with plastic surgery, personal trainers and chefs, and airbrushing demanded in their contracts.

That's why I've started showing pictures of naked men and women in my counseling sessions, which have been taken especially for sex therapy to show clients that most people sag in certain places and that breasts and nipples can be different shapes and sizes. For most people, there is a huge sense of relief to compare themselves to normal people rather than to models or movie stars. However, I would like to go a step further. Instead of just tolerating our imperfections, I think we should celebrate them and even consider them sexy. But how do we get there?

*"Instead of just tolerating our imperfections,*
*I think we should celebrate them and even consider them sexy."*

1. *Stop putting yourself down.* One of the ways that women bond with other women, or make themselves seem less threatening, is listing their faults. Worse still, it soon gets into a contest where everyone claims to hate themselves the most. Although this sort of behavior will make you feel like a member of the clique, it does nothing for self-confidence. Next time, simply refuse to enter the competition, walk away, or change the subject.

2. *Stop putting other people down.* Entire magazines are devoted to famous women's flaws with circles pointing out their "muffin tops," "panty lines," and "cellulite." We imagine that by putting celebrities down to our level, we'll somehow feel better about ourselves. However, it just feeds our own fears that we will never measure up.

3. *Stop imagining that a good body equals confidence.* I've twice been in the company of someone so overwhelmingly good looking that heads turned only to learn that he or she was the most self-conscious of all.

4. *Not everybody wants to go to bed with someone gorgeous.* The great American novelist Norman Mailer married a woman half his age. His wife, Norris Mailer, discovered that he was being unfaithful to her with women who were either closer to his age (by that point he was almost seventy) or significantly overweight. When she asked him why, he replied, "Sometimes I want to be the attractive one."

5. *Celebrate your achievements.* We've all done things we are proud of. It might be knocking three minutes off your personal best for running a half marathon, closing a deal at work, or having the courage to tell your mother you'd like to host the holidays this year. Transfer that small moment of internal pride into a proper celebration by having a bottle of sparkling wine in the fridge ready or reward yourself with a special treat.

6. *Remember a time when you did feel confident.* Picture in detail the last time that you did feel good about yourself—it could even have been in a lucid dream. Anchor that experience by remembering where you

were and how good it felt. Think about where the confidence seemed to come from: your stomach, heart, head, hands, etc. Next, imagine moving it around your body so that every part is filled with confidence and raising and lowering the volume. Once you have a solid grip on the feeling, you can trigger it whenever you need it. Start by using this trick somewhere nonthreatening (but potentially troubling) like a difficult meeting at work, and then progress up to feeling confident in the bedroom.

7. *Does it really matter what other people think?* Barry, thirty-eight, came into counseling because he had no confidence when meeting women. "I'll be talking to someone and suddenly I'll be gripped by the thought, *She's thinking about my nose, how big it looks, that it's huge, and dominates my whole face, the whole room.*"

Barry had been using the strategy of celebrating his achievements to cope. "I tell myself, *I've started a good business, it's doing really well, and I'm going to start to employ more people.*"

As Barry had been having these thoughts even when dealing with low-stakes situations, like talking to someone in the office down the hall from his company, I asked, "Does it really matter what they think?"

During the next week, he had been able to ask himself the same question whenever he'd starting worrying about his nose. "It really helped get everything into perspective. Why should I worry about someone whose good opinion I don't need?"

By acting quickly, when the nasty internal voice started up, he'd headed off the problem and prevented himself from plunging into obsession.

8. *Make peace with your body.* Instead of promising to accept your body when you've lost a pound or have better pecs, accept yourself as you are today. This doesn't mean abandoning your health and fitness goals. You still want to eat well and partake in moderate exercise, but stop putting off doing things until you've reached some magical target.

## SOMETHING TO SLEEP ON

**In summary, remember:**

- You need to prepare yourself for a richer love life by becoming more aware of your senses (rather than hurrying through your to-do list) and more in touch with your feelings (rather than ignoring them because they are troubling or inconvenient).

- We spend far too much time worrying about our looks and what people think about us.

- Confidence is incredibly sexy.

# SEX ED

### EXERCISE 7    SETTING ASIDE TIME FOR EACH OTHER

No relationship can thrive on snatched moments for very long. The following ideas will help you set aside time for each other and create the platform for improved lovemaking.

**Live mindfully.** Over the next week, observe how much time you spend together in the same room or space. So although you might both be home on Saturday morning, if one of you is in the garage and the other in the kitchen that does not count. How much of this time is "business" contact—by that I mean arranging what time to pick up the kids or what time you'll be back for supper? How much of this is "leisure" time, and by that I mean chatting about this and that (rather than giving each other instructions or passing on information), sharing pastimes, socializing with others, or just hanging out together?

**Reassess your priorities.** It is easy to fall into the trap of putting our partner last. We imagine that he or she knows that we truly love him or her and therefore will not be hurt if we spend two hours on the phone to a friend in crisis. There are so many little things that need to done, he or she will understand if we just wipe down the kitchen surfaces or make that work call. We tell ourselves that our partner is an adult and therefore can fend for him- or herself, while our sons and daughters need our attention. We forget that children are just passing through, but a partnership is forever. Have you been taking your partner for granted?

**Realign your lives so they intersect.** Rather than making ambitious changes (like date night), which can easily be derailed, develop good habits that provide regular opportunities to be together. Intimacy or in-depth conversations cannot be scheduled; they arise naturally out of chunks of shared time.

For example, when you get home, seek out your partner and chat about your day. If you're home first, put down what you're doing for five minutes and give your partner your undivided attention when he or she arrives. Make a commitment to share meals together (without the television on). Go to bed at similar times, so your body clocks are in synch.

### EXERCISE 8    MAKING AMENDS FOR THE PAST

Until you can cooperate, it will be hard to work as a team to improve your sex life. The following will help you achieve this goal and put the past behind you.

**Acknowledge past problems.** The more something is not spoken about, the more power it accumulates. We talk about the elephant in the room as something everybody is aware of but which everybody ignores. However, the Dutch have a better saying that really encapsulates the idea: "A dead horse on the table." It's right under our noses, and the longer we ignore it, the greater the smell and the greater the problem. By contrast, speaking the truth is like opening a window. Not only does the smell dissipate, the horse can be given a decent burial.

When acknowledging a problem, you don't need to rehash what happened or explain why something hurts. In just a sentence or two, make certain you own the feelings ("I am still hurting from your affair" or "I find it hard to get along with your mother") rather than blaming someone else ("You hurt me when you cheated" or "Your mother has never accepted me"). The first version simply reports your feelings and invites a discussion, while the second makes your partner defensive and encourages an argument.

**Apologize for your share.** However blameless you might feel about the origins of the problems, look at your contribution to the impasse. There is probably something that you regret, however minor. For example, staying with the previous example, "I'm sorry that I took you for granted" or "I shouldn't have lost my temper with your mother as it made things worse." Don't add explanations, as these can seem like excuses and reduce the power of the apology. In addition, the power of saying sorry can be magnified by acknowledging how your behavior affected your partner: "And that made you feel unloved and alone" or "and that made you feel pulled in two directions." A fulsome apology—when you express sorrow, accept your part in the problem, and demonstrate that you understand the impact of your behavior—will encourage your partner to make a similar move.

**Forgive your partner.** There are three attitudes that make forgiveness harder.

First is that forgiveness will let a partner off the hook (which would be true only if you give instant forgiveness without understanding the underlying causes or seeking to solve them).

Second is the idea that a partner might commit the crime again (but does your constant disapproval and anger help to mend bridges or just keep the two of you apart?).

Third is the thought that a partner does not deserve forgiveness, and if this is how you truly feel, you are not ready to work on your love life.

(Read my book *Resolve Your Differences: Seven Steps to Dealing with Conflict in Your Relationship* first.) After having looked at what forgiveness is *not* about, let's focus on what it really means. If forgiveness is truly given and not coerced, it allows you to let go of resentment, blame, and anger. Therefore, forgiveness is not just an act of generosity to your partner but a gift to yourself. It frees you from the past, allowing you to draw a line in the sand and start fresh.

**Ask for what you want.** Often we are frightened of being rejected, so we drop hints or hope our partner will *know* what we need.

Alternatively, when we do ask, we lessen the impact of a simple straightforward request ("I'm going to bed now; will you come up too?") with preambles or explanations ("We've been having a lot of late nights recently, and I think it's important that we get a good rest . . .") that invite discussion, argument, or cause our partners to turn off. Sometimes we are so focused on building consensus that our partner is handed a ready-made "opt out" clause ("I know you're watching this program . . .").

If this sounds difficult, practice asking in low-risk situations (like at work) or request things on which your heart is not set so rejection will not be too painful.

**Recruit your partner into my program.** Use the lessons from this exercise to get your partner on board. Acknowledge past problems: "I know our love life has been a bit predictable, and although we enjoy it, we never seem to get around to it."

Apologize for your part: "I've left you to make all the first moves" or "I've often been too tired." Forgive your partner: "I used to be resentful because you would sulk if you didn't get sex, but I've decided to put that behind us and start again."

Ask for what you want: "I've bought this book with a weekly program to improve our sex life. Please read it, so you can understand the underlying philosophy."

# Chapter Four

# A Month of Sensuality

When I ask couples who are dissatisfied with their lovemaking whether they cuddle, they are normally quick to dismiss the idea. Sure, of course they cuddle. Doesn't everybody? However, when I question them further, their cuddle is seldom more than a quick hug in the morning or accompanying a kiss goodnight. And how much time does the average couple spend together? According to the Office of National Statistics, it is very little. Once work, commuting time, sleep, and media have been deducted from a normal week, all that is left for couple downtime is three and a half hours a week. That's just twenty-four minutes a day!

*"Once work, commuting time, sleep, and media have been deducted from a normal week, all that is left for couple downtime is three and a half hours a week. That's just twenty-four minutes a day!"*

In the rush to get through our to-do list, deal with the latest demands from work, the children, or the many other competing priorities for our time, we tend to boil everything down to the bare minimum. However, if you want to be on the same emotional wavelength and have connected sex, it takes time to unwind and tune in to each other. That's why I've put longer cuddling and sensual touch at the heart of my program.

In a nutshell, I'm going to strip your sex life back to basics, check for bad habits (which diminish desire), give you enough time to discover what turns you on today (rather than when you first met), and then slowly build back your lovemaking in a way that puts passion and feeling at the center.

How I start this journey is a puzzle to many couples who come to me for counseling or attend my workshops. The best way to put the spark back into your love life is to stop having sex. I can hear them thinking, *Hang on a second, we sought help because we're hardly ever making love, and now he's going to stop us altogether? How can we ever improve if we don't have a chance to practice?* But before you cast the idea aside, let me explain more.

There are three reasons for putting a ban on intercourse and other forms of sexual contact. First, it significantly reduces tension between couples. Second, it helps couples get in touch with the full range of sensual pleasures rather than rushing toward an orgasm. Third, it can change the way that you communicate. I know these are bold claims, so let's look at how banning sex reestablished the relationship of Mike and Jenny from the previous chapters.

Mike had been so eager to make love that he applied emotional pressure. "I couldn't stand Mike sulking, so after a while, I'd give in to what he wanted," Jenny explained, "and I'd just lie there like a sack of potatoes."

Mike did not find this sort of sex satisfying either. He would prefer Jenny had been an active partner. He looked glum. I asked him what he was feeling, but he couldn't put it into words.

"Is it better than nothing?" I prompted.

"No, it is worse than nothing because I'm still frustrated," Mike replied.

Between these unsatisfactory bouts of sex, there was virtually no physical contact between Mike and Jenny.

"I wouldn't mind a cuddle, but I don't want to send out the wrong signals," said Jenny.

Mike and Jenny had fallen into a nasty trap common in many couples with unhappy love lives—*all or nothing*. They either had full intercourse or stayed at opposite sides of the bed. There was no sensuality, no togetherness, and no intimacy in their marriage. Had they continued down this path, Jenny would probably have closed down completely and started to refuse sex.

By agreeing to a ban on sex, by which I mean no intercourse, oral sex, or masturbating together, Mike and Jenny could start fresh. Jenny could relax and enjoy a cuddle without dreading a sexual encounter she wasn't up for. And, instead of hoping *maybe this time,* Mike could also enjoy the moment. In effect, they would return to being teenagers, enjoying heavy petting as a pleasure in its own right, instead of a quick warm up for intercourse. (I will explain the rules of what contact is permitted and what is off-limits in a moment.)

When they returned the next week, they were both smiling. The tension and the arguments had significantly reduced, and they had cuddled every night after their daughter had been put to bed.

"I felt so much closer to Jenny. It was nice to be held, but it was even nicer to be able to show my love for her," Mike explained. There had also been a significant breakthrough in their general communication.

"I don't like it when he surprises me from behind. If I'm in the kitchen, I'm in my own world, and although he is just being nice and giving me a hug, I go all cold inside," said Jenny. "I hadn't told him this before, because I didn't think it was important, but my last boyfriend tried to strangle me on several occasions. Although I'm not frightened of Mike, if I don't know he's there, it brings back memories."

Mike had known that her boyfriend had been rough but had no idea of the degree. "It also explains why she hates being kissed on the neck," he said. These revelations not only brought the couple closer but shone further light onto understanding their problem.

> *"By agreeing to a ban on sex, Mike and Jenny could start fresh. Jenny could relax and enjoy a cuddle without dreading a sexual encounter she wasn't up for."*

The intimacy of the cuddles had another positive effect: Mike and Jenny were more relaxed and spent more time together. Over the weekend, they took their daughter to play in the park, and Jenny stepped aside to give Mike time to play with her. They were behaving more like co-parents instead of Jenny taking the lion's share of their daughter's attention. As he talked about his daughter at the counseling session, I could see two competing sides of Mike. There was the brash builder who I could imagine joking with his friends and the more sensitive man who loved his wife so much that he was jealous of the way their child came between them. So I encouraged Mike to talk about his own father:

"He was a good man. Firm but fair," he explained.

"Did he show his feelings?" I asked.

"Real men don't show their feelings," he joked.

Unfortunately, Mike's upbringing and his hyper-masculine work environment had cut him off from expressing his tender side. His only "socially acceptable" channel for communication was having sex (because "real men" are also "studs"). By closing down this option, with a ban on intercourse, oral sex, and masturbating together, he began to look for other ways of showing his feelings. At this point, it was just a glimmer, but the beginning of something very important.

## BAN INTERCOURSE, INDUCE INTIMACY

This four-week "sex diet" sets out to repair and rebuild the loving bonds between you and your partner by shifting the emphasis from reaching orgasm to touching, caressing, and holding each other. As you read the following weekly activities, think about them and discuss with your partner whether there is anything that makes you uncomfortable and, if this is the case, make any necessary adjustments. It is fine to stay with one activity for a second or third week, so don't rush ahead if you don't feel ready.

When working with clients on this program, I always say I expect there to be some weeks when they don't do their "homework." So please don't make achieving each week's goal a test of whether your partner is truly committed—that just ups the stakes and makes it harder to cope with setbacks. In fact, most people get stuck somewhere along the way. It's partly because life happens—family comes to visit or one partner is ill—but changing the habits of a lifetime and facing our demons is tough. It is fine to extend the sex diet by a couple of weeks.

Please be kind to each other, discuss what didn't work, try again, or go back to where you felt comfortable. What matters is not how quickly you progress but how you deal with any obstacles. If you think of a setback as a learning opportunity, you can't go wrong.

## WEEK ONE:  Focus on Cuddling and Sensual Touching

Flip a coin to decide who will go first. The winner becomes the first person to say, "I would like to be touched." (I would like you to do this exercise twice during the week, so the next time will be the other person's turn to initiate.) The winner can immediately say, "I want to be touched" or wait for a convenient moment over the next few hours or days. As long as the person asking to be touched does not pick an incredibly inconvenient moment like in the middle of cooking dinner or bathing children, the other will put down what he or she is doing.

- Go somewhere warm, quiet, and private.

- The touchee lies down and the toucher explores the touchee's body. (If you would rather keep your underwear on that's fine.) The only forbidden areas are the genitals and the breasts as well as sensitive areas that relate to some sort of trauma from your partner's past.

- It is not a performance, so don't worry about technique. Really enjoy looking at your partner's body. Let your feelings flow. (Don't be surprised if some unexpected ones like sadness surface.)

- Discover what kind of touching gets the best response. Does firmer pressure or really light touch work better? What about scratching the back? Mix up the sensations.

- The touchee should provide plenty of feedback but avoid talking (as this can sometimes be interpreted as criticism). If something feels good, don't keep it to yourself. Let out a sigh or a moan of pleasure. If your partner's touch is too firm, raise his or her hand slightly. If the touch is too light or tickles in an unpleasant manner, gently push your partner's hand downward.

- After fifteen minutes, switch turns. The touchee becomes the toucher.

- End with a cuddle. Remember sex (intercourse, oral sex, and masturbating together) has been banned for the time being. Discuss the experience and your reactions (especially the unexpected ones).

- Later in the week, the other partner is the person to initiate by announcing, "I would like to be touched," and the whole exercise is repeated.

## WEEK TWO: Focus on Kissing

My plan is designed to add a layer of sensuality each week, so continue with the same activities from week one, taking turns. Beyond a peck on the lips, many couples abandon sensual kissing in the rush to have an orgasm. With that distraction temporarily out of the way, you can really focus on enjoying kissing again.

- Start with the original script: "I would like to be touched."

- After a few minutes of sensual touching, look for new places to kiss your partner. What about the neck or the elbow? (Remember genitals and breasts are still forbidden.) Don't just go for obvious places to kiss like the lips; try others like the belly, fingers, and armpits.

- Alternate the kissing with sensual touching, so your partner is not certain what sensation will be next.

- Experiment with different kinds of kisses. Butterfly kisses land really gently and can come in quick succession. Slobbery kisses pull lots of flesh into your mouth. Nibbling kisses involve a light use of the teeth.

- The touchee remains in control. If it is unpleasant to be kissed somewhere, she or he can move their partner's head. Give plenty of moans and sighs, so your partner knows what is particularly enjoyable (but don't put on a performance; this has to come naturally).

- Toward the end of your fifteen minutes of sensual touching and kissing, try kissing on the mouth. Open your eyes, so it is a very personal experience.

- Once again, alternate between different kinds of kisses on the lips and with tongues.

- After fifteen minutes switch.

- Like before, finish with a cuddle and offer feedback to your partner about what you particularly enjoyed.

# FRENCH KISSING

Teenagers spend a lot of time worrying about the art of French kissing (or *baiser amoureux* in French), but adults forget how good it feels. Worse still, many couples only French kiss before intercourse. For example, Jenny, from earlier in the chapter, had removed French kissing from her repertoire for fear of sending "the wrong signals."

So this task works in tandem with the Month of Sensuality. After week two, when you have started sensual kissing, bring kissing out of the bedroom and incorporate a good French kiss into the rest of your life together. (I find this works particularly well with couples like Jenny and Mike where housework, childcare, and chores eat up the majority of shared time together. A French kiss is a good way of checking back in with each other and remembering that you are lovers.)

So what's the secret of a good open-mouthed kiss?

*Moisten your lips.* Dry lips do not move well together. No need for lip balm, just a light brush of your tongue over your lips. (It can also look quite sexually provocative.)

*Mix it up.* Alternate deep kisses with shallower ones; concentrate on stimulating the lips. Remember, the tongue is very sensitive and light touching with the tip is particularly stimulating.

*Use your hands.* Cup your partner's face, caress his or her shoulders, and wrap your arms around each other. Once again, find lots of different ways to touch, but do not go for the breasts or genitals.

*Keep going.* A good French kiss should last for at least two or three minutes. Allow enough time for the passion to rise, so it is not simply a social kiss hello or goodbye.

*Stop and talk.* The idea is not to progress to making love, just end by giving your partner a compliment, positive feedback ("I really liked it when you. . .") or say, "I love you."

*Repeat.* It will take a while to break the habit that French kiss = sex. So experiment with different places and times to French kiss. If you are uncertain whether you should make an advance, ask your partner.

## WEEK THREE: Focus on Advanced Sensual Touching

Combine this week's activity in conjunction with the sensual touching and kissing exercises from the two previous weeks, except the allotted time is now twenty minutes, but preserve the ban on intercourse, oral sex, and masturbating together. With advanced sensual touching, different sensations are elicited by adding fabrics (for example, a piece of velvet, silk, or faux fur) and other ordinary items that you have lying around the house. (I've had clients who have enjoyed pastry brushes, feathers, and even fine sandpaper.)

- Have a look around your house and see what you can improvise with. Alternatively, a craft shop, the supermarket, or your local hardware store will be full of ideas. Some couples find it pleasurable to surprise each other, while others enjoy the buzz of a shared shopping expedition.

- Vary the different sensations and give each other plenty of feedback about what feels nice.

- There is another new element this week: the breasts.

- About five minutes before the end of the woman's sensual time, she should guide her partner's hands to her breasts. By this point, she will be comfortable showing what feels nice and what doesn't. She should make certain her partner knows what works for her by getting his hands to shadow hers (verbal feedback is still off-limits).

- When it's the man's turn to be touched, around five minutes before the end, he should also guide his partner to his nipples toward the end of the twenty minutes. Just as in the female's anatomy, men possess several nerve endings in the nipple area, so this can be a possible new source of pleasure. Try out different techniques—licking, nibbling, tweaking, and even gentle pulling can be pleasurable. Start slowly and build up the intensity.

- Remember, you are still not allowed an orgasm. If you sense your partner is heading into this zone, stop and wait for him or her to calm down and then start again. (It might seem cruel, but your partner will find it intensely pleasurable to be taken to the edge of a climax only to be left hanging.)

- Finish with a cuddle and a discussion about what worked and what didn't and which fabrics or household items to discard and which ones should find permanent homes in the bedroom.

## WEEK FOUR: Focus on Simultaneous Orgasm

Once again, we are staying with the twenty-minute time frame, but this week, you may finish the touching exercise with an orgasm. Begin with sensual touching, progress through kissing, and lead to advanced touching. The ban on intercourse and oral sex is still in effect, but each partner can simultaneously masturbate *themselves* for the other to see. Many couples think this is the opposite of intimacy, and many are shocked by the idea. However, sharing what, for many, is a secret activity can promote a profound connection.

- Maintain good eye contact. Watch how your partner pleasures him- or herself, so you can use this information later in the program.

- Masturbation might feel too revealing or private to share with your partner, but as you will discover, holding too much of ourselves back results in boring sex.

- Pushing past the taboo of masturbating yourself in front of your partner is what makes week four such a spectacular climax—in every sense of the word—to a Month of Sensuality.

## SOMETHING TO SLEEP ON

**In summary, remember:**

- Raising a family, earning a living, and running a household is so tiring and stressful that we can demote lovemaking to the bottom of our list of priorities. Unfortunately, this can make our partner feel unwanted or unimportant.

- Cuddling and sensual touch can begin to repair this damage, as one can never be too tired to be held or stroked.

- The first weeks of my program put a ban on sexual intercourse to channel all your communication into an experience of touch, to stop you from repeating the same old mistakes, and to strip down your lovemaking before building up to something better and more fulfilling.

- By taking direct stimulation to each other's genitals temporarily out of the equation, you will become aware of other centers of pleasure in your body.

- In addition to the sense of sight, bring all your other senses—touch, smell, taste, and sound—into the bedroom.

# SEX ED

## EXERCISE 9    TURN YOUR BEDROOM INTO A SENSUAL SPACE

I often ask my clients to describe their bedrooms, and in some cases, it is amazing that any lovemaking happens there at all. One couple had a dog that slept in a cage by the bed, so when it yelped in the middle of the night, the husband could reach over and give the cage a knock.

- **Unclutter your bedroom.** Look around your bedroom with fresh eyes. Has it become a dumping ground? Are the items on the bedside table like flu remedies, folders from work, and household bills conducive to lovemaking? What about pictures? Do you really want snapshots of your children or parents on the wall?

- **Create the right atmosphere for lovemaking.** Many bedrooms can be a bit feminine (pink, flowery, and lots of pleated fabric) or child-like (stuffed animals). What sort of sexual energy does this create? Is there anything present that might inhibit one or both of you? How could you make this a more neutral place in which you can both project your sensuality?

- **Is your bedroom warm enough?** Nothing is less conducive to good lovemaking than being cold. Do you need to upgrade the radiator or get a heater for instant warmth?

- **Improve the lighting.** Scientists have discovered that making love exclusively in the dark or with harsh artificial lighting deprives us of a natural sexual stimulant to the brain—the pineal and pituitary gland—which are vital for arousal. Try to create natural and soft full-spectrum lighting in your bedroom.

- **Use music as sound proofing.** Installing a sound system in the bedroom is another good tip for reducing your fear of being overheard and for creating the right mood. Choose music with no strong theme, vocals, and changes in beat. Making up your own sexy compilations can be fun and much better than the radio.

· **Stimulate all your senses.** Don't overlook the importance of smell. This can range from opening a window for fresh air to scented candles, air ionizers, and incense. Think of everything possible to stop your bedroom from being the "bored" room.

## EXERCISE 10    THE IMPORTANCE OF MASTURBATION

It is vital to know your body and what gives it pleasure; otherwise, how can you communicate effectively with your partner? That's why, since the birth of sex therapy in the 1950s, masturbation has been part of the learning phase.

I've put a ban on intercourse and oral sex throughout the Month of Sensuality (and have prohibited masturbating together for the first three weeks) because I don't want you to rush toward an orgasm. However, I'm aware that it's hard to go for such a long time without the comfort and release of an orgasm, which is why I do allow *private* masturbation on your own throughout my entire program.

Private masturbation is a difficult topic for many. When I first began working as a marital therapist almost thirty years ago, few, if any, couples I counseled had discussed it. It was too private, even with a partner! In fact, there was also a double standard. It was accepted that men masturbated but assumed that women didn't. These same men hated the idea of their wives masturbating alone. It was almost as if they felt cheated. If their wives wanted sex, they only had to ask. The idea that their wives should be allowed to please themselves seemed alien. Although we live in more enlightened times, many women still feel guilty about private masturbation.

Therefore, I set the private masturbation exercise for two different reasons: to offer sexual release, so neither of you breaks the no orgasm rule of the first three weeks of the Month of Sensuality, and to learn more about pleasing yourself. If you seldom masturbate on your own, I'd like you to experiment at least once. If you regularly masturbate, you are free to do so as often as you wish.

You need to honor this exercise. By this, I mean setting aside enough time to get in the mood, rather than accessing porn and simply "getting off." (If you are a regular porn user, please take a break, so that your mind is not full of secondhand images and scripts.) Maybe you would like to have a bath, put on some music, or light a candle. In the words of Woody Allen, "Don't knock masturbation. It's sex with someone I love."

- Empty your brain of day-to-day clutter. If you find it hard to switch off, concentrate on the sensation of the air going in and out of your nose.

- Start to caress yourself and explore your body with your hands, partly to help yourself relax but mainly because this is the opportunity to have just the amount of foreplay you need to prepare for sexual touching.

- Only when you are truly ready should you fondle your genitals and build up to masturbation.

- What images, shapes, pictures, ideas, stories, or scenarios float into your mind? If you have tried lucid dreaming, there might be material there that you could use. Allow time for sexual thoughts to establish and develop. Enjoy yourself. Afterward, think about what you have learned about yourself.

- For further understanding of the nature of fantasies, read Nancy Friday's *My Secret Garden: Women's Sexual Fantasies* and *Men in Love, Men's Sexual Fantasies: The Triumph of Love Over Rage*.

# Chapter Five

# The Great Desire Debate

In my initial interviews with couples, I ask both parties their perspective on their love life. In most instances, the man says he wants more sex so he can feel "close" to his partner, while the woman says she doesn't want to have sex until she feels emotionally "closer" to her partner. It almost seems like the old chicken-and-egg scenario. Does sex create more closeness or closeness more sex? Settling this great desire debate is a major part of solving intimacy issues and creating a sex life that is mutually satisfying.

When one partner feels pressured to have sex or the other cut off from it, nothing good can come out of it. Take Simon and Cassie. "I'm worried that we're drifting apart," Simon told me as he sat next to his wife of fifteen years, Cassie. "We used to make love about once a week, although I would have liked more, but more recently it's like I have to beg to make love to my wife. If we have no togetherness, how can we move forward?"

Cassie saw the situation differently. "But you don't pay any attention to me. Unless you want sex, you don't talk or listen to me." Because, like most men, Simon responded better to stress, he imagined that Cassie would also respond to his pressure to make love. So if they went for more than ten days without sex, he dropped unsubtle hints (disguised as "jokes"), sulked, or didn't cooperate around the house. Not surprisingly, this strategy had turned her off. In contrast, like most women, Cassie rated quality time together as most important to induce bonding.

Of course men do feel close to a woman when they share their feelings, hold hands, and hang out together. However, in my experience, in order to bond nonsexually, the average man needs *twice* as much nonsexual "togetherness" as the average woman. Conversely, if you throw physical touch into the equation—stroking, cuddling, and sexual foreplay—he will feel close within *half* the time of his mate. So although he is fine with the idea of "spending more time together" or "opening up his heart," he imagines hours and hours of talking and longs for a more direct route.

Women, of course, feel close to men when they have sex. However, they have a million and one other ways to feel bonded—through raising children together, caring for each other, or going out—so women would not necessarily be concerned if their marriage went through a phase where they hardly had sex at all. Although the average woman is definitely up for more frequent and better sex, she doesn't believe her whole life would fall apart if the quantity dropped because she would still feel connected to her partner via alternate ways. While typically I have found that women are fine with the idea of spicing up their sex lives, they tend to believe that as soon as they experience "mind blowing" sex, men will ignore them again.

With such different ways of perceiving sex and bonding, it is important to stress what men and women have in common. They all want to feel desire (because it makes them feel young, potent, and alive), and they all want to be desired (because it makes them feel validated, important, and attractive). That's why my program is designed to bring couples together in ways that appeal to these different expressions while still creating the spark of desire.

## THE MYTHS OF DESIRE

We're constantly monitoring our levels of desire. On a first date, we might ask ourselves, "Do I like this guy?" When we're in a long-term relationship, we might ask ourselves, "Do I want to have sex?" We tend to treat desire for sex as if it were an on-off switch, but it is not such a black-and-white issue. Unfortunately, the gray parts of the debate have been shut out because of some pervasive and faulty cultural ideas about desire. So what are these myths and how do they make it harder to maintain a healthy sex life?

## Desire Is Natural

Technically, desire is a biological tool used to propagate the species. It manifests itself in humans as a craving for sexual pleasure, as something inherent to our personalities, like scratching an itch or relieving tension (Freud's idea of libido or sex drive) or part of being human (John Stuart Mill, the nineteenth-century British philosopher, who believed that we seek pleasure and avoid pain). There is nothing wrong with any of these ideas, except they locate desire in the reptilian part of our brain at the top of our spinal column, which controls basic functions like breathing and digestion.

Alicia, thirty-two, couldn't find love. Her relationships had either been intensely passionate (but with little or no common interests) or based on friendship (with little or no sex). She had just ended one of her passionate relationships. "Jake has been very good for me. He made me feel attractive and desirable again, and when you've got a small child, that's no small feat. But I know he's not right for me. Every time I try to end it, he calls me and convinces me to meet him for a drink. When I see him, there's this craving inside, and I can't keep my hands off him. Obviously, we end up in bed, even though I know I'll feel terrible the next morning."

On the other hand, the father of her child, Howard, had been one of her "friendship" relationships. "I really respect him, and he's helped my career by being a mentor and opening doors. I liked him so much that I thought I should be attracted to him too, and I talked myself into giving it a try, and that's how we accidentally had a child together." Unfortunately, Alicia did not see any future in the relationship because Howard did not turn her on. They split up before their baby was born.

Like many single people, especially those whose parents divorced when they were young, Alicia expected what I call "big bang sex" to bind her and her partner and launch them into a lifetime of loving togetherness. Unfortunately, big bang sex had bonded her to inappropriate men and made her overlook others with whom she could have had a lasting and fulfilling relationship. Maybe if she could have gotten over her fear of being hurt and of repeating her parents' mistakes, she could've opened her mind to the idea that desire sometimes takes time to build. Maybe she could've stayed with Howard and the first sparks of connection, if properly tended, could have been fanned into a flame.

Long-married couples also fall victim to the "desire is natural" myth and become vulnerable to affairs. After all, we're forever being told that natural is best—natural food, health products, fabrics—so if we feel passion for someone other than our partner (and we believe desire comes naturally), shouldn't we follow it? When Frank was forty-six and had been married for twenty years to Gwen, he met Lucy at work. "There was an immediate connection, something I hadn't had with my wife for years. We tried to fight it, but the passion was stronger than the both of us. We'd meet up and I'd be ready to end it, but we'd start kissing or she'd slip her shoes off and rub her foot up my thigh and I'd be lost. We did split up once or twice, but we couldn't keep away from each other."

> *"Long married couples also fall victim*
> *to the 'desire is natural' myth."*

Inevitably, someone saw Frank and Lucy in a wine bar and sent an anonymous text to Gwen. When the affair was discovered, Frank was forced to choose and left his wife, who was devastated. When Frank came into counseling six years later, regret had set in. "Secretly, I think I made a big mistake, but I can't go back because Gwen is happily remarried and my daughters tell me they're a great match. Sometimes I wonder if Lucy sent that anonymous text to force my hand."

So although you might believe that in an ideal world desire should come naturally, I would like you to challenge this myth and find a more nuanced position. Instead of seeing desire as something free-floating and independent of you, recognize how it is influenced by your thoughts, your feelings about your partner, and the general stresses in your life, all of which you have the ability to influence and change.

## Sex = Intimacy

Sex is one of the ways we communicate and reflects our longing to bond with one another, but when this myth permeates a relationship, it tells the couple that the amount and quality of sex is a barometer of the health of the relationship.

This function of sex places desire in the mammalian part (the midsection) of the brain, which controls anxiety and the fight-or-flight response. However, while nothing brings us physically closer to another person than sexual intercourse, it is not the only way to measure intimacy. Time and again, I counsel people who close their eyes to the true state of their relationships because they are still having regular and reasonably satisfactory sex.

By the time Maddy and Mitchel arrived in my office, they were in crisis. After fifteen years of marriage and two children, Mitchel had told Maddy he didn't think he loved her anymore and that he'd been feeling that way for a long time. Unfortunately, this had come as a complete shock to Maddy, who responded, "But less than six months ago, we took off to that ski cabin and had two wonderful weeks. We must have made love every day in every room of the cabin."

"Sure, it was nice," Mitchel said. "I enjoyed the sex too, but I didn't really feel any connection."

As the counseling continued, we discovered that although Mitchel and Maddy had been physically close during that vacation, he had not felt emotionally close.

"We always do things your way," admitted Mitchel. "You chose which restaurant we had to go to and met your girlfriend and her husband there. If I suggest a place, you get all uppity because it's not gourmet."

In effect, while they had been physically intimate, Mitchel did not feel free to share his feelings, thoughts, or opinions.

## THE TRUTH ABOUT DESIRE

Desire does have a natural or biological component, but we can regulate our impulses in the brain. After all, even if we find someone incredibly attractive, we have the will to not copulate with them in the street (like dogs). Being intimate is an important ingredient for desire, but a straight link between actions and how we feel de-emphasizes the importance of the roles our brains play in how we interpret events.

For example, Margaret, fifty-three, and Joseph, fifty-five, sought help after Joseph had an affair while on a business trip. After a lot of talking, soul searching, and two months of counseling, the couple was closer than they had been in years. "We just have this little sex problem," explained Margaret. "About twenty-five percent of the time that we're making love, Joseph will lose his erection."

"How do you react?" I asked.

"It doesn't happen when I'm giving him oral sex but sometimes when he's returning the favor. So naturally, I'm angry and hurt and want him to stop. I roll over and try to go to sleep."

This is how Margaret viewed her desire:

$$\text{Event} \longrightarrow \text{Feeling}$$
$$\text{Losing erection} \longrightarrow \text{Rejection}$$

However, I wanted to know what was happening in her head. When I asked her why she felt rejected, she replied, "He didn't lose his erection when he made love to *her* [the other woman]."

"How do you know that?" I asked.

"I don't know for certain, but he's told me that the sex was good, so he must have been aroused."

Margaret interpreted Joseph's lack of erection as a personal rejection that told her she wasn't good enough for him.

"She was almost twenty years younger, and if I'd been enough in the first place, he wouldn't have strayed," she continued.

Although it was painful to connect the dots, we now had a more accurate picture of why Margaret felt rejected.

$$\text{Event} \longrightarrow \text{Interpretation} \longrightarrow \text{Feeling}$$
$$\text{Losing erection} \longrightarrow \text{I'm not sexy enough} \longrightarrow \text{Rejection}$$

Next, I challenged her interpretation of events.

"So your husband's affair was all because you are not attractive enough?" I asked.

"No, of course not. He was away on business and would get lonely and my father was ill, so I'd been preoccupied with him."

"And when you're giving Joseph oral sex, where is your focus? On his body or your own?"

"On his body, of course?" Margaret was puzzled.

"So you're not focused on your vagina and how lubricated it is? You're concentrating on your husband's pleasure."

Margaret nodded as she realized that Joseph might be concentrating on her when he's pleasuring her.

I went on to explain that even for men in their twenties, erections and desire come and go during lovemaking. Men in their fifties will often need more stimulation to become physically aroused, and it is not a reflection of how much they love or desire their partners. Finally, men of any age who become anxious about their erections will find it more difficult to perform, regardless of how they feel about their partner.

Event $\longrightarrow$ Interpretation $\longrightarrow$ Feeling

Losing erection $\longrightarrow$ Natural part of lovemaking $\longrightarrow$ Unconcerned

By acknowledging the role our thought processes play in creating or impeding desire, we acknowledge the part of our brains that makes us human, the neocortex, located in the forehead. When it comes to placing meaning onto sex beyond the biological urges, we are alone in the animal kingdom. This is what makes intimacy and sexual desire so incredibly complicated, because except for a few exceptions, it matters to us what we or are partner is feeling physically *and* emotionally.

In other words, desire has three important ingredients:

Touch

Thoughts

Feelings

Sex is possible with just one or two of these qualities present. For example, touch alone can provide a stimulating but probably meaningless one-night stand, or someone might have "just get it over with" sex with their long-term partner. However, all three ingredients need to be working together for passionate and fulfilling lovemaking.

# DESIRE INHIBITORS

Whether a couple is equally dissatisfied with the quantity or quality of sex or have fallen into a routine or have given up totally on the idea of rebuilding a sex life, there is still hope. Moving away from the black-and-white attitude of desire is something you either feel or don't, it's possible to recognize the everyday culprits that keep you and your partner inhibited.

## Performance Anxiety

A small amount of anxiety and uncertainty can be catalysts for pleasurable lovemaking. Hence the relative ease of sex with someone new or make-up sex after a fight. However, high levels of anxiety like "Am I doing this right?" or "Will she know I'm inexperienced?" or "Does he think I'm fat?" can kill even the most accomplished touch and prevent desire. Worse still, anxiety is contagious. If one partner is anxious, the other will become anxious too, and a vicious cycle ensues.

Lesley, twenty-eight, had always been worried about making love. "Sex was never talked about in our family, but there was an unspoken message that I should be a virgin on my wedding day. I suppose this was somewhere in the back of my head because whenever things between my boyfriend, Gavin, and me headed toward sex, I would tense up."

Although nothing was said, Lesley's body language was communicating loud and clear.

"I was really worried about hurting her," said Gavin. "I thought I was doing something wrong and put it down to being young and clumsy and ignorant."

So Gavin would either lose his erection or make a half-hearted attempt at penetration. Instead of talking about their individual worries and how they fed off each other, they "managed" their anxiety by avoiding intercourse altogether.

Time and again, I counsel couples that are anxious about whether they are "good enough" in bed. Men's anxiety tends to focus on whether they can "satisfy" their partner and women's anxiety tends to focus on their bodies. Unfortunately, rather than talking about these fears and releasing the tension, each partner will find coping strategies such as turning off the lights or focusing on technique rather than on the other person. Ultimately, neither partner winds up being really present while they are making love. And if you're only half there, the sex will only be half as good and little opportunity is created for desire to flourish.

## Unresolved Emotional Issues

If you are not talking about something important outside the bedroom, it is unlikely you will be connecting inside. Although many couples blame their lack of desire on communication problems, all too often they are communicating very effectively. After all, there is nothing clearer than a turned back or absent sex. Both actions convey the message "I don't want to get close." What people mean by "communication problems" is not that they haven't been able to talk about their problems, but that they have not been able to *resolve* their differences.

> *"If you are not talking about something important outside the bedroom, it is unlikely you will be connecting inside."*

When Sarah, twenty-eight, fell in love with Jeremy, thirty-seven, she accepted that he had been married before and had a seven-year-old daughter. Although she got along with the daughter, Sarah objected to the way Jeremy's ex-wife interfered with their lives.

"She'll call at the last minute and change the time or day we can pick up Jeremy's daughter, which completely disrupts our plans," explained Sarah.

Jeremy didn't think the problem was so serious. "I've tried to lay down the law more with my ex, and she has been a lot more considerate recently."

Sarah nodded her head, and although I wondered if the subject was closed, we focused on other issues (mainly helping Sarah and Jeremy argue constructively) as well as on their low levels of desire. Although both committed to the Month of Sensuality (see Chapter Five), there were lots of plausible excuses, but no progress. When they had only managed half of week one's exercise, in which Jeremy had initiated the touching, I suspected they had unresolved emotional issues. In fact, in the next counseling session, everything came to surface.

"I'd gone to pick up something I'd left at work, so I wasn't home when Jeremy's ex came to pick up their daughter. The arrangement was that she wouldn't come into our house, as I don't like the idea of her snooping around my home because she's in our life enough already," explained Sarah. "You can imagine my surprise when I returned and found her in my kitchen."

Jeremy was trying to be calm, but it was obvious that they'd been over this a million times already. "We were talking about summer vacation, and I needed to check something on the calendar. It seemed easier to figure it out then and there. It was only a minute."

I suddenly had a picture in my mind of Sarah and Jeremy making love and Sarah feeling as if Jeremy's ex-wife were sitting at the end of the bed. So I asked Sarah, "Is Jeremy's ex-wife inhibiting your desire?"

"I don't feel safe enough to let go," said Sarah in a quiet voice.

So we stopped working on their love life and concentrated on resolving this issue. Several weeks later, when Sarah had not only attended her stepdaughter's birthday party at Jeremy's old house but enjoyed the occasion, the desire returned and Sarah and Jeremy were able to graduate from my program with a passionate and fulfilling love life.

It is not just unresolved emotional issues between the couple but each partner's individual problems that can inhibit desire. Angela, twenty-eight, had been living with her partner for five years and although their sex life was "okay," she wanted to be able to relax and truly enjoy their lovemaking. Even a couple of weeks into working together, when most people have gotten over their natural reserve and embarrassment over talking about sex, I sensed that Angela was still holding back. So I talked about the protective barriers that everybody uses to stop others from taking advantage and asked how high hers were at that moment. Angela pointed to her forehead, while her partner, Adrian, pointed to just above his waistline.

"I know I should be able to trust you," Angela admitted to me, "and Adrian too, but I find it hard to let myself go and be vulnerable."

"It seems like you're having trouble letting go of your desire too and becoming sexually needy because it would not only reveal your vulnerability but risk rejection."

Slowly Angela talked about the legacy of having a father with Asperger's syndrome and how, when he was stressed, he'd explode irrationally in anger. It had left Angela wary and highly defensive at even the least hint of discontent.

Once I'd helped her become more aware of her barriers, when it was appropriate to raise them and when not, she found herself able to relax more in bed and the couple's lovemaking improved.

## Fused Sex Lives

The next scenario that inhibits desire comes as shock to many couples who think being close is an asset. However, it is possible to be so close that it can spoil your lovemaking, either by turning you into brother and sister (the opposite of feeling sexy together) or being so responsible for each other's sexual happiness that you're overwhelmed. After all, it's hard enough to negotiate your own sexual hang-ups without being responsible for your partner's too. So what exactly do I mean by "fused"?

In every relationship, there needs to be a healthy balance of both *we* and *I*. Too much *we* and the couple loses track of their individual identity, while too much *I* means there is no relationship (just two people sharing a home). Meanwhile, we might love our partner and want the best for him or her, but we can't run his or her life and we're certainly not his or her therapist.

Caroline and David were in their late thirties and had been together for over fifteen years when they entered counseling for their low-to-no-sex relationship. They lived in a small apartment, both worked from home, and David was helping Caroline launch a business. However, it was not just their business lives that were fused. Whenever Caroline got stressed and upset, she would unburden herself to David. "I had a difficult childhood. My parents split up when I was a teenager, and my mother married a man who I hated, so I can easily get overwhelmed and let it all out."

There's nothing wrong with sharing a problem, but for Caroline it normally came out as a torrent with one problem sparking another.

"The other day I was worried about a problem with the business and how hard it was to work together, and if we can't work together, how could we cooperate and have children? What if our whole relationship is doomed?"

After an hour of pouring out all her fears and escalating worries to David, Caroline felt much better. Unfortunately, David, who, up to that moment, had been doing all right, became overwhelmed and sank into a depression. Like many fused couples, Caroline and David let their own and each other's anxiety undermine their relationship.

Fortunately, there is an alternative: taking responsibility for your own feelings and learning to self-soothe rather than expecting your partner to come to your rescue. This does not mean keeping your feelings to yourself. It is fine to report your feelings, for example, "I'm feeling low and stressed," but avoid dumping on your partner, for example, "Nothing ever goes my way," "I can't cope," "I'm never going to finish," and so on. While reporting keeps your partner informed, dumping risks "infecting" your partner with your anxieties and stress.

When Caroline was unable to soothe her own anxieties and center herself on her own, David felt obliged not just to listen but to take on all her problems and solve them.

"When Caroline is upset, I get upset, and it starts a vicious cycle because I get more and more stressed," says David. "Perhaps she's right. If we can't figure out an accounting system for her business, perhaps we *are* doomed. I'm trying to solve the account's problem and our whole relationship at the same time, so I'll get snappy or likelier shut down and walk away. It's the only way I can process everything."

In fact, David found it just as hard to self-soothe as Caroline. Instead of being able to tell himself that he loves Caroline but is not responsible for every detail of her life, he became infected by her anxiety and resorted to blanking out.

So how does a fused relationship create problems in the bedroom? In David and Caroline's case, they would worry so much whether the other was having a good time that neither could relax and enjoy. Worse still, their relationship was so important, and they were so frightened of each other's disapproval, that it became almost impossible to experiment with sex. The resulting sexual boredom further exacerbated their low levels of desire. However, once Caroline and David learned to self-soothe and stabilize their own fears on their own, they stopped being overwhelmed or infected by each other, and their desire quickly returned. (I will explain more about self-soothing and the differences between healthy and unhealthy ways to cope in a moment.)

Another example of a fused couple with sex problems is Craig and Nicola, who are both in their midtwenties. When they did make love, it was pleasurable and rewarding. Unfortunately, it happened only once every six weeks. The more they talked, the more fused they sounded, until I had a picture of two people sharing genitals.

When I asked Craig if he ever masturbated alone, especially since they had sex so seldom, he was quite shocked. "I think that would be very selfish, and, anyway, if I satisfied myself, I'd probably have even less desire."

Nicola, who was generally responsible for initiating their lovemaking, would often playfully grab his penis if he came out of the shower, especially if he had an erection. "I'm never certain if she's just kidding around, so I tend to freeze up."

Meanwhile, Nicola would complain that when they cuddled, Craig would go straight for her breasts. "He hasn't said as much, but it's like he thinks he's entitled, and that's a big turnoff."

Over the course of their counseling, Craig and Nicola learned to express their different needs and become less fused. Not only did they start to follow different interests without feeling guilty about not sharing everything, their sex life also started to improve.

## THE ART OF SELF-SOOTHING

When children fall over, whether it really hurts or not, they burst into tears and one or both of parents run over and "kiss it better." One of the most important parts of growing up is learning how to self-soothe instead of expecting someone else to lift us up. Unfortunately, self-soothing is one of the hardest things to achieve, and the myth that "love will solve everything" encourages us to expect our partners to step into the role that our parents once held. The whole concept of soothing is further complicated because there are constructive and destructive strategies.

**Destructive Ways to Soothe:**

*Blanking:* This strategy includes denying there is a problem, shutting down, or rationalizing away everything.

*Self-medicating:* Using alcohol, recreational drugs, work, etc., to distract attention from underlying problems or manage stress.

*Dumping:* Instead of taking responsibility for your own problems, you expect others to come to your rescue (and then get angry when they don't rise to the challenge).

*Acting Out:* When children have problems at home—for example, parents divorcing—they often "act out" their problems by being disruptive in class or taking their anger out by bullying smaller or weaker pupils. Adults act out by losing their temper over something trivial, driving too fast, plotting revenge, etc.

**Constructive Ways to Soothe:**

*Acknowledging:* Sit quietly and become aware of the feeling and what it is trying to tell you.

*Processing:* When the feeling is strong, or induces panic, concentrate on your breathing, inhaling through your nose and exhaling out of your mouth. When you are calmer, assess the problem and what can be done about it. Going for a run or walking the dog can similarly help process and understand the feelings. Once you have processed the feelings and isolated the relevant issue, your partner is likelier to listen rather than be overwhelmed by a pile of problems.

*Engaging:* If you cannot find an immediate solution, where can you get information or advice? Think about your specific needs. For example, if the car has been broken into, think about contacting the police, your insurers, and a glass repair company, rather than dumping the problem on your partner.

*Reporting*: Keep your partner and loved ones informed of your feelings ("I'm tired" or "My boss is a nightmare and I'm at my wit's end"), so they don't feel excluded or imagine they've done something wrong. It also invites your partner to offer help, advice, or support.

*Choosing*: Ultimately, reaching out to your partner becomes a choice, not a necessity. When it is a large problem—like bereavement, unemployment, or serious illness—it may be sensible to ask for your partner's help to soothe.

## WHAT PROMOTES DESIRE

At the beginning of a relationship, lust almost hardwires us into the arousal stage, so we don't need to be aware of desire and how to feed it. We just magically fall into each other's arms. By the time the honeymoon period finishes, most couples have to work at bridging the gap between day-to-day life (the pressures of earning a living, running a house, and bringing up children) and the desire stage (the sensual world of love-making). Unfortunately, the couples who depend on just lust are left stranded, frustrated, and blaming each other, mostly because they cannot bridge the gap between the mundane reality of being a couple (which includes diapers, laundry, and bills) and the bliss of sex. When I counsel couples to build bridges from their less passionate selves to feelings of desire, I begin by reminding them of how passion builds and the four phases through which it travels:

1. **Desire** (positive anticipation and feeling that you deserve sexual pleasure)

2. **Arousal** (being receptive and responsive to touching and intimate stimulation)

3. **Orgasm** (letting go and allowing arousal to naturally culminate in pleasure)

4. **Satisfaction** (feeling emotionally and physically bonded after a sexual experience)

In order for a couple to experience these phases in a way that fulfills and connects them, desire must first be present. Therefore, the tools I give to my couples are called Bridges to Desire, which enables them to shift gears and literally bridge the gap between "not in the mood" to "interested" and onto "can't keep your hands off."

*Bridge 1: Casual Touching.* The most important bridge to desire is casual touching—for example, holding hands in the street, a neck message while watching TV, or nibbling each other's ears. Casual touch is the bedrock for a healthy love life because small acts of affectionate contact help people feel desirable and allows couples to unwind and get on the same emotional wavelength. The good news is that if you have completed and enjoyed a Month of Sensuality, you have already added this bridge to your repertoire.

For Mike and Jenny, whom we met earlier in the book, casual touch had been a revelation. "I really enjoyed having the pressure taken off," said Jenny. Previously, she would have had to decide if she was aroused the moment Mike first touched her, but now they had a proper bridge to desire. They could either enjoy the non-demanding touching, which is pleasurable by itself, or decide to have sex.

*Bridge 2: Plan.* While every couple enjoys the first bridge from everyday life into lovemaking, the next one is always more controversial. When I tried to convince Adam and Hannah, who are in their late twenties, that sex needs to be planned, Hannah argued that sex is better when it's spontaneous and natural.

I agree, but those qualities alone cannot sustain desire.

Adam was more pragmatic, stating that anticipation made for increased desire and therefore more pleasure. "Remember when I got those tickets for U2. We looked forward to that for ages, and somehow it made the evening even better."

Indeed, anticipation is important for building desire. After I probed further into Hannah's worries about a "sex date," she asked, "But what if I'm not in the mood?"

This is important because feeling obliged is a barrier, rather than a bridge, to desire. Fortunately, they had completed their Month of Sensuality, and Adam agreed that cuddling and fondling would be enough intimacy in the event Hannah did not want to go further.

"We stayed in, and I cooked us a nice meal. Adam had downloaded some new music and we danced in the living room and one thing led to another. Actually, it felt quite natural," explained Hannah.

*Bridge 3: Play.* For couples who feel self-conscious about planning ahead, I often include another bridge: Play. When we were children, play was at the center of our lives. Play was a gateway to learning, team building, and an opportunity to let off steam. All of these qualities are just as important for pleasurable lovemaking. Unfortunately, as adults we forget how creative and how much fun playing can be. So I've instructed couples to have food fights, ride the seesaw, or play tag. These games break down barriers and help partners see each other in a new light, which is ultimately very sexy.

*Bridge 4: Flirt.* Similar to play, flirting, whether through teasing each other, assigning pet names, telling jokes, or giving compliments, can be a solid bridge. In effect, you are giving each other a packet of sexual energy and seeing if the other returns it.

*Bridge 5: Provide Distance.* This bridge from the practical to the passionate is a surprise to most couples: good lovemaking needs distance as much as closeness. Charlotte and Edward, in their fifties, had not made love for over six months and described themselves as best friends. "I always know what Edward is thinking," claimed Charlotte. "She's right. She does," agreed Edward. They did lots of things as a couple—fine dining, a busy social life—but very little apart.

"We hold hands when we go shopping, and he's very considerate . . . opening doors, but I wish . . ." Charlotte drifted into a sad silence.

"There are more important things in a marriage," Edward quipped.

I doubt that's what Charlotte meant, but she smiled in agreement. Instead of being two individuals, albeit in a relationship, they had become one amorphous couple who was frightened of allowing each other to be different. The first step was to encourage them to argue more, which is the quickest and most effective way to release submerged passion. Next, I asked them to witness each other's separate lives.

Edward went to a conference where Charlotte was speaking. Charlotte watched Edward play tennis, an interest he'd given up when their children were young.

"I really admired how he really went for each shot, and he looked sexy in his shorts too," Charlotte said, blushing.

"And I saw the respect of Charlotte's colleagues," explained Edward. "It was like seeing her through a new lens." Soon after these experiments, Charlotte and Edward reported passionate lovemaking again. It is when we see the distance between us and our partner, and recognize each other as a separate person who is independent of us, that we understand there is enough space for desire to return.

Ultimately, there are many ways to bridge desire, inspire connection, respect, communication, and love for one other. Cooking a meal together or giving an acknowledging glance across a room at a party, appreciating one's "love language," giving a tickle as you pass your partner while putting the kids to bed, or so many other seemingly innocuous events and acts can be bridges to desire. However, here are some tips to get the most bang for your bridge.

- Use different bridges at different stages in your relationship.

- Don't use the same bridge over and over. Bridges wear out, get old, and become less reliable for building a sensual life.

- Have a variety of possible bridges and choose the most appropriate one for the occasion. (For example, when you've lots of time, you might like to use "casual touch," but if you're going through a really busy patch, you might find "planning" works better.)

## WHAT HAPPY COUPLES KNOW

Over the years I have studied what common denominators are shared by couples who report increased desire and fulfilling sex life and have identified five:

1. *Investing time.* If sex is the last thought of an exhausted mind and the last act of an exhausted body, it is unlikely to be inspiring. My sexually successful couples prioritize enough time together to tune in to each other. In particular, female clients attribute a session of good lovemaking to feeling "really relaxed."

2. *Self-validation.* If you rely on other people as the prime source of feeling attractive, sex can become not an expression of love but proof that you are desirable. Worse still, over time, your partner's praise becomes less and less effective because "he would say that, wouldn't he?" or "she's just saying that because she has to," while the interest of strangers becomes more and more powerful (making you vulnerable to an affair). While people who need others to validate them are a black hole and suck the sexual energy out of a relationship, people who are secure in their own skin and like themselves emit sexual energy.

3. *Good eye contact.* No wonder the women in all cultures use makeup to draw attention to the eyes. Good eye contact is important for initiating sex and shows that someone is truly present in the moment. Sexually successful couples keep their eyes open during foreplay and communicate how they're feeling and direct their partners and monitor how the other is feeling.

4. *Being in the moment.* Sexually successful couples clear their mind of other concerns and worries, and are therefore aware of the feelings building in their body. (If you have an overactive mind, see the exercise section for advice.)

5. *Good communication.* It is important to share thoughts and relevant feelings, so if there are problems or something needs to be changed, both partners know they will be listened to and their concerns taken seriously.

# SO, YOU THINK YOU'RE READY FOR SEX AGAIN

Tread carefully. The aim of a Month of Sensuality was to make you aware that your whole body is a source of pleasure—not just the breasts and genitals. And hopefully this lesson on the Great Desire Debate helped you understand that there are two sides to the story. It is important to listen to your partner and take his or her thoughts and beliefs about sex into account, even if they are different from yours.

If you just skip from a Month of Sexuality right to intercourse, you're going to miss one of the best parts of creating lasting pleasure and desire. I call it Two Weeks of Wickedness.

# TWO WEEKS OF WICKEDNESS

Up to this point, I have been asking you to focus less on your genitals as a source of pleasure, but now they are about to take center stage. Some people find this rather uncomfortable, particularly if they prefer their lovemaking under the covers. Stephanie, forty-two, grimaced when I outlined this next task. "It all sounds dirty." To which I quoted Woody Allen: "Is sex dirty? Only if it's done right." By this I mean you have to make peace with and enjoy every part of your body before you can surrender yourself to being passionate.

### WEEK ONE: Show and Tell (Part One)

- Before you start touching each other's genitals, you need to look at them—*really* look at your own.

- Stand naked *alone* in front of a full-length mirror. If you don't have a mirror that shows at least head to knees, it's probably time to buy one.

- Take a full inventory of what you *like* about your body. Say it out loud or write it down. This is a hard task partly because we have been trained from childhood not to be conceited, and partly because we only see images of "perfect" bodies in the media (which have been airbrushed or altered). Women find this task difficult, especially if they bond with friends by putting down parts of their own or other women's bodies.

- Look again at your reflection and aim to find five good things. For example, Stephanie reported, "I have a cute belly button and my bottom has a nice curve but . . ."

  I could tell she was about to add something negative, so I stopped her. This is not about what could be changed or improved. It is five things that you like. Finally, Stephanie added her nipples, her fingers, and her long neck. She started crying. "That's probably the first time I've ever looked at myself without adding 'but.'"

- Next focus on your genitals. For men, look at your perineum (the sensitive ridge between your anus and scrotum). Cup your testicles and feel their weight. Roll back your foreskin, if you have one. Look at the tip of your penis, squeeze it, and watch how it (the urethra) opens and closes. For women, spread your *labia majora* (the outer lips of your vagina) and peer inside. Pull back the vaginal hood from your clitoris and examine it as closely as possible. A large number of women, like Stephanie, go through life without examining this sensitive spot. (A hand mirror might help.)

## WEEK ONE: Show and Tell (Part Two)

- Later in the week, the two of you should stand *together* naked in front of the mirror.

- Flip a coin to decide who talks first. The winner goes through all the things about her or his body that she or he likes. Talk about your genitals too and show some of the discoveries. Maybe you will need the hand mirror to show the more intimate or overlooked parts of your bodies. Give your partner a tour, preferably with a running commentary.

- Don't worry if this is not remotely sexy. The aim is to introduce your partner to every inch of your body, and your genitals are just another part of the body no different from, for instance, your knee.

- Look carefully at how your partner handles his or her genitals. This will provide clues for the future for what she or he enjoys.

- Switch turns. When you are both finished, the first person goes again, giving compliments to the other. Looking in the mirror, tell your partner, "I've always liked . . ." or "I never knew how beautiful your . . ." Fill in the blanks.

- When given a compliment, don't knock it down. Just thank your partner and return the positive feedback.

- When you have finished, give each other a hug and get dressed.

- Discuss what the experience was like and reveal what surprised you about your partner's comments.

## WEEK TWO: Focus on Arousal

- The touchee lies down and the toucher explores the touchee's body. The only forbidden areas are the genitals and the breasts. Kissing will also be the same as last month, in that you may kiss on the mouth and nonerogenous zones.

- After ten to fifteen minutes, begin to explore your partner's genitals and emulate how you saw your partner touch him- or herself.

- Take your time. This is a sensual pleasure, not a means to an end. Alternate different kinds of touching: Firm. Light. Tips of fingers. Quick. Slow. In circles or up and down, or in and out. (The touchee is still in control. If something is too intense, she or he can wordlessly move the toucher's hand or press down/pull up to vary the pressure.)

- Allow enough time to experiment (up to fifteen minutes) alternating touching genitals with other parts of your partner's body.

- Don't worry if your partner does not have an erection all the time or if her vagina is not constantly lubricated. The penis is still sensitive when flaccid, and so is the vagina when not engorged.

- Switch places, so the toucher becomes the touchee.

- Focus on your arousal and how it flows and ebbs. Enjoy the moment. Intimacy does not have to end just because the penis is not constantly erect.

- Finish with a cuddle rather than an orgasm so that you focus on your journey and not just the destination.

The main lesson of Two Weeks of Wickedness is to notice how desire comes and goes, even when you're in the thick of sexual engagement. Men, in particular, are focused on whether they have an erection or not and forget that the penis is still sensitive while flaccid or semierect. The fear of losing potency makes men rush through sex and focus on reaching orgasm rather than on their feelings. Women also worry that when they lose desire, it is gone for the evening, or give up when unable to climax within some self-imposed time limit. This task will offer proof that erections and desire fluctuates but come back, especially when there is no fixed goal.

## SOMETHING TO SLEEP ON

**In summary, remember:**

- One of the biggest barriers to a fulfilling love life is the belief that sex should be "spur of the moment" or come "naturally." The ideas of an "instant fit" and "chemical compatibility" make it harder for single people to forge deeper and lasting connections and can bond them with unsuitable partners. It also encourages long-term couples to wait until desire sweeps them away.

- Desire needs three ingredients: touch (an animal connection), feelings (a heart connection), and thoughts (a brain connection).

- Couples need to find a balance between being too independent (and having no relationship) and becoming fused (where each partner's sense of themselves is reflected through the other's eyes). The goal is to become interdependent.

- Knowing how your genitals look and work, while feeling comfortable sharing them with your partner, are important ingredients for good lovemaking.

# SEX ED

## EXERCISE 11    A NEW RECIPE FOR DESIRE

Many people think of desire as something that they feel or don't. If they are in the mood for sex, great. If they're not, oh well. However, I prefer to think of desire as being like a cake. You might go to the cake plate and find someone snatched the last piece that you had your mind on the entire day. But, if you have the recipe and know where to find the ingredients, you can soon bake a fresh one. A cake needs eggs, butter, flour, sugar, and water, so what ingredients does desire need?

When I asked Rosemary, forty-two, this question, she came up with the following ingredients, beginning with the most important:

- Content in the relationship
- Feel secured and cared for
- Interest in the person
- Attraction
- Meaningful compliments
- Feeling appreciated
- Time together
- Playful touching
- Prioritize play more

In just the same way as there are hundreds of different types of cakes requiring a variation in ingredients—chocolate, carrot, red velvet, cheese—there are hundreds of different types of desire, with a multitude of ingredients that can be combined to create a happy sex life. Write down and tailor your list of ingredients and ask your partner to write down his or hers. What are the differences? What are the similarities? Finally, how can you support each other's desire?

## EXERCISE 12   HOW TO CONJURE DESIRE

We are so misled by the idea that sex and romance are dependent upon spontaneity that we are in denial about how much planning goes into being "spontaneous." To see a clearer picture:

1.  Look back at your most recent "natural" lovemaking moment.

    - What facilitated the right mood? (For example, arranging for the children to be out, booking a table at a favorite restaurant, jetting away to a romantic destination.)

    - How much preparation? (For example, wearing the right clothes or washing or personal grooming.)

    - What other ingredients went into creating the "spontaneity"? (For example, the bottle of champagne you threw in the fridge or the music you downloaded or the florist you called.)

2.  Add up the number of phone calls, emails, purchases, and decisions that went into being "spontaneous":

    - How do you feel about this result?

    - Who does the majority of the organizing?

    - Is it you or your partner? How does that make you feel?

3.  By relying on chemistry or some unspoken magic to carry you into the sensual world, you are not taking responsibility for your own lovemaking. So ask yourself:

    - What is stopping me from owning up to how much I need and enjoy sex?

    - What messages have I received from my parents, friends, and society/culture about sex?

    - Off the top of your head, complete these sentences. When it comes to sex, nice girls _____. When it comes to sex, good boys _____.

- How could responsibility for lovemaking—initiating, planning, and arranging babysitting—be more evenly shared? Looking back at your answers, what changes would you like to make to your behavior?

## EXERCISE 13    HOW TO PLAN INTIMATE TIME

Now that you've accepted that spontaneous sex and romance are not all they're cracked up to be, you can take responsibility for creating desire in yourself and inspiring it in your partner. Of course, spontaneous lovemaking is wonderful, but if you wait until both of you just happen to be in the right mood, at the same time and in the right place, you can end up waiting a long, long time. Alternatively, a little planning can solve all these problems.

When I set up this task, my clients are skeptical: "What if I'm tired?" "I don't want to feel like I have to," or "Isn't it all a bit clinical?" First, there is no obligation to make love, only to be physically intimate. You could have a bubble bath together, slow dance to a favorite song, or get out a bottle of body oil and give each other a massage. Second, setting aside time for each other is proof that you value each other. Once alone together, your mood will probably change. (It's a bit like going for a meal and not being particularly hungry until you arrive at the restaurant and look at the specials.) Third, I am not suggesting that all your lovemaking is preplanned, but planning must become one of your bridges to desire.

Here are a few guidelines for your sex date:

- Mark the calendar.
- Set aside at least an hour, preferably more.
- Agree that the date does not have to end with an orgasm, although it would be welcome. (If you are sticking to my program, which I advise, and if orgasm is planned, it should occur through solo masturbation in tandem.)

- Make arrangements so that you will not be disturbed. (If you have teenage children, you might like to book a hotel room or arrange for them to sleep over at a friend's.)

- Think of ways to make your time special. What about favorite foods? How could you create a loving atmosphere?

- The more energy you put into your date, the more enjoyment you'll get out of it. After all, you reap what you sow.

## EXERCISE 14    SWITCHING OFF A SPINNING MIND

Many people find it hard to disengage their brain, let go, and notice when they feel desire. Some cannot relax until all the chores have been done, and others are too busy churning over the events of the day or particular problems. They are like a hamster on a wheel, constantly running but getting nowhere. So what's the alternative?

- **Accept that overthinking is counterproductive.** There comes a point when further ruminating just confuses or promotes bad decision making.

- **Unload your thoughts.** When left to go around and around in your brain, thoughts and jobs-to-do get bigger and bigger. So put everything down on paper, as if you are taking dictation from your brain—don't censor or edit, just get it down.

- **Review your thoughts.** First of all, you'll be surprised that there is less on the page than you might have expected. Look for words like "should" and "must" and question the beliefs. For example: "Why must you clean the kitchen before you make love?" Who says? Where does this belief come from? Is this belief right? Look for statements that are simply not true and cross those off. For others, be like an investigator and look for the evidence for the "facts" on your piece of paper.

- **Put off coming with up a solution or doing that "must-do" job.** Having accepted that most pressing tasks are no such thing, put off, for example, checking emails or tidying up until later. In the same way, put off thinking about a pressing problem. In many cases, you will have forgotten the problem the next day.

- **If the problem returns, simply push it away.** If you begin to make love and a thought pops into your head (for example, "We're out of coffee"), imagine pushing it out of your brain (rather than thinking "I could pop into the supermarket on my way back from work tomorrow"). You will be surprised how easily these thoughts disappear if you don't allow them to take hold. If, however, you find this technique difficult, consider meditation classes and train your mind to be still.

# Chapter Six

# The Three Sex Styles

Over the past five chapters, you have understood more about your and your partner's attitudes toward sex, have repaired any damage caused by miscommunication and the stresses of modern life, and have begun to deepen your bond. This chapter is aimed at maintaining your progress and preventing you from slipping back into bad habits.

"On the face of it, our sex life is fine. We make love, typically once a week, and it's okay," explained Claire, forty-five, who came alone for her first session. "Except, it makes me feel even more distant from Derek. Sex seems to be another box to check off. *Great, that's over, what's next?* We don't seem to connect, and I'm feeling lonelier and lonelier. It didn't use to be like this."

The more Claire talked, the more I saw two bored people going through the motions. Lovemaking doesn't have to become boring. We get bored in the bedroom because we get scared. Our partners learn so much about us from living together and raising children that to share too much more feels like being swallowed up. Alternatively, we worry that if our partners knew the real us that they wouldn't like us anymore. So we show less and less of ourselves until we become, in our partner's eyes, a one-dimensional caricature rather than a fully rounded individual.

Neuroscience can explain not only why we are so convinced that our partner will never surprise us again but also a way forward to solve this dilemma. The brain's job is to make sense of the world, and generally, it likes to simplify and find one solution. And this often happens in the left hemisphere of the brain. However, when there are multiple potential interpretations offered by the right hemisphere, fortunately the brain has the ability to meet the challenge and hold all these ideas at the same time.

For example, Vermeer's masterpiece, *Girl with a Pearl Earring,* is one stable image. However many times you look at this painting, it will not move or change. Yet because there are lots of different, but equally valid, interpretations of the expression on the girl's face, this picture continues to fascinate us three hundred and fifty years after its creation. The girl's look is both inviting and distant. Her eyes seem both sexually charged and chaste. She appears resentful yet pleased by our attention. Vermeer's genius is that he managed to convey all these expressions at the same time. Academics are still debating whether the pearl is real, the significance of the turban, and the identity of the girl.

In contrast, pictures with a single interpretation might hold our attention for a moment, but however beautiful, they are seldom worth a second look and we soon lose interest. The secret to sustaining your love life, therefore, is to present yourself to your partner in all your complexity—not just your love and understanding but also to trust him or her with your fears, jealousy, and darker side.

*"The secret to sustaining your love life is to present yourself to your partner in all your complexity."*

## TWO WEEKS OF VARIETY

The aim of this part of my program is to include more variety in lovemaking and allow you to see your partner in a new light—as the multidimensional, wonderfully mysterious, and complex person you are, as is the *Girl with a Pearl Earring.* As you have already learned through a Month of Sensuality and Two Weeks of Wickedness, this program relies on breaking the habit of a myopic view where only full genital intercourse counts as *real* sex. For many couples, this is the only destination, which creates two problems.

First, knowing how something ends is not only predictable but also promotes boredom. In movies, they call this a "spoiler," and I can't think of a better word to describe it regarding sex. Second, the stakes are raised, and initiating lovemaking becomes riskier. In the split second after one partner starts fondling the other's thigh, or whatever signal for sex is used, the other partner has to make an instant calculation. *Does he or she want sex? Can he get an erection? Can she be bothered?* More times than not, the answer is no. And all of this inner chatter takes away from the moment, and being in the moment is one of the catalysts of desire.

However, if a hand sneaking across the bed is an invitation to a range of sexual possibilities, from cuddling to intercourse, the chance of a positive response is significantly increased. Across the next two weeks that comprise Two Weeks of Variety, you have the opportunity to extend your range of sexual options.

## WEEK ONE: Different Strokes

- Start with the previously discussed combination of sensual pleasuring and kissing, with one partner being the toucher and the other, the touchee.

- When the touchee feels ready, he or she should start to play with his or her own genitals, demonstrating what he or she likes.

- The toucher puts his or her hand over the touchee's, to help understand the rhythm and style that is most enjoyed.

- After a couple of minutes of shadowing with the toucher's hand over the touchee's, the toucher takes control and masturbates his or her partner.

- Experiment with different ways to give your partner pleasure, slow down and drive him or her wild, then speed up and increase the intensity.

- Finish off by giving your partner an orgasm, if he or she wishes, but treat an orgasm as an optional extra rather than the goal of this exercise.

- Switch places and repeat.

## HAVING AN ORGASM WHILE YOUR PARTNER IS WATCHING

One of the contradictions of loving sex is that the better you know someone, the harder it is to let go and surrender to the pleasure. After all, your partner knows all the other versions of you (like being a mother or father, a competent responsible person who holds down a job, a member of your local community or church, etc.), and this makes it embarrassing to reveal your lustful, animal side. Research has shown that only 15 to 30 percent of couples have sex with their eyes open. Some people find it helps them concentrate on their own pleasure, especially during the buildup to an orgasm, and, for some, that means deliberately zoning out their partner. I doubt anyone *wants* to shut out their lover, but otherwise, it just feels too intense, too revealing, and too embarrassing.

So while you may find it difficult to have an orgasm while your partner watches, especially for women who have received more negative messages about sex than men, the act allows you to be 100 percent intimate with your partner because you are revealing a private part of yourself. Inhibition is what drains the excitement out of long-term relationships. To help you overcome your trepidation, I offer the following suggestions.

- Close your eyes. It's fine to not keep your eyes open most of the time. Do play peek-a-boo occasionally and look at your partner for a second or two for a flirty and fun experience.

- Concentrate on your breathing to promote relaxation. Breathe deeply to fully expand your lungs, letting the air out slowly.

- Place a large mirror in your bedroom and watch each other masturbate in it. In this way, you are creating an illusion that you are watching someone other than yourself, removing yourself from the picture as if you were an entirely different couple.

- Blindfold your partner and give him or her a playful running commentary about what you're doing to yourself and how it feels. (You might even like to pretend that you're someone else.) Don't keep the feelings inside. If something feels good, let out a sigh or a moan.

- Talk to each other as a way of distracting yourself. Complement each other or communicate your love or offer something a little saucier.

**WEEK TWO: Oral Sex**

Some people find oral sex a problem because they are worried about cleanliness. So this week start in the shower together. Spend time soaping each other down, washing each other's hair, and washing each other's genitals. This last part allows you to ensure that your partner is clean, but showering together can also be fun in its own right.

- If you are the toucher, start with pleasuring your partner's whole body before fondling his or her genitals.

- Some couples build up to oral sex by garnishing each other's genitals with fruit or ice cream. Making love should not always be such a serious business!

- When receiving oral sex, the touchee can guide his or her partner's head but do not give verbal feedback, as this can be misconstrued as criticism.

- If the touchee wishes, you can finish by giving him or her an orgasm orally or, if you prefer, manually.

- Switch places and repeat.

In the early stages of my program, you escaped from "all or nothing" by enjoying cuddling for its own sake, which helps with the stress of twenty-four hour life as you're seldom too tired for kissing and cuddling. Once into this sensual world, you could be ready for much more, and with the Two Weeks of Variety, you have added extra sexual destinations and the foundations for delving deeper into what you both enjoy. After you have completed these exercises, you are ready to remove the ban on intercourse, if you have not yet done so.

## THE THREE STYLES OF LOVEMAKING

In the fifties, William H. Masters and Virginia E. Johnson began their groundbreaking research recruiting couples to have sex in their laboratory and monitoring what happens to their bodies during orgasm. However, it was not until the late seventies that psychologists began to look at the meanings we place on lovemaking and what separates functional sex (where someone orgasms) from rewarding sex (which is emotionally satisfying as well as physically).

Professor Donald L. Mosher, from the University of Connecticut, was the first person to scientifically study what went on inside people's heads. He based his theories on what was already known about how the brain responds to hypnosis and asked recruits to fill out detailed questionnaires about their attitudes toward sex. Mosher identified three different ways that couples make love. I have taken his work, updated it, and expanded the ideas in my work with couples over the past thirty years.

My clients find the identification of three styles of lovemaking a particularly helpful tool because it provides a framework to explain to each other what each enjoys, but also acts as inspiration for exploring other sexual possibilities. Before I lay out the concept, it is important to say that one kind of lovemaking is not inherently superior to another but dependent upon your particular personality, your sexuality (what you find sexually pleasing), your experiences to date, and which outside messages about sex you may have adopted. So what are these three kinds of lovemaking and how can they help keep committed sex passionate?

## Trance

In this style of lovemaking, the focus is inward-looking and centered on either giving or receiving pleasure. Someone engaged in trance sex drifts into his or her own private world. If there is talking, it is normally to give instructions or feedback. If there are any fantasies, they are normally without a script but full of sensual images, colors, and shapes. For people who enjoy trance lovemaking, sex is an altered state of consciousness or being transported to a different planet.

"I love to sink into lovemaking and relax into a world where the colors are brighter and more focused," explains Janine, thirty. "Sometimes I'm lying on a warm beach with the waves lapping at my feet or running through the woods, faster and faster, until all the leaves float off the trees."

Slow pacing and repetitive movements (round and round, up and down) help people who enjoy trance lovemaking relax and let go. The ambience is incredibly important. Sensitive lighting, warmth, and music all help create a calm and peaceful mood. However, the most important ingredients are privacy and no outside distractions (like children coming home unexpectedly). This style of lovemaking is affectionate and about mutual pleasure. The perfect orgasm involves intense sensations and losing track of both place and time.

Pillow talk or being asked questions prevents trance lovemakers from surrendering to their feelings. Sometimes, they can find kissing on the lips too invasive because it pulls them back to reality. They don't enjoy sex games and find it hard to share their fantasies as they are often visual, wordless, and almost hallucinatory.

## Levels of Trance

One of the most inspired parts of Mosher's theory is that there are not only three styles of lovemaking, but also each one has several levels (which I have distilled down to five). When I discuss these levels with my clients, there is a natural desire to head for the highest one (as if sex were an Olympic sport), but I always stress that there are advantages to each and every level. So what are the five levels of trance?

- *Casual:* You are relaxed enough to shut out everyday concerns (e.g., the ironing and checking emails) and have begun to interpret your partner's gestures as sexual (so that a touch or a look becomes erotic or romantic rather than consoling or friendly).

- *Routine:* Reality begins to fade away (rather than making a conscious effort to shut off). Both partners are focused on sex instead of kissing and cuddling. The awareness of the world around—critical for everyday survival—is relaxed as you become more receptive to pleasure. However, it is still easy to be distracted by a noise downstairs or suddenly remembering something you need to do.

- *Engrossed:* You have completely abandoned everyday reality and begin to sink down into the trance. Nothing short of a knock on the door or your car alarm going off will stop you now.

- *Entranced:* At this level of trance, you and your partner might be in separate worlds, but the connection is so strong that there is no division between giving and receiving pleasure or touching and being touched. You are locked in a loop where your partner's pleasure increases yours and vice versa. Only someone shouting fire will stop you from reaching orgasm—and maybe not even that!

- *Ecstatic:* There is total absorption in the trance. All the boundaries disappear. The connection is not just with your partner but with every lover in the world (and maybe throughout all time). Sex has reached an almost spiritual level and the need for an orgasm fades into insignificance.

## HOW TO GO DEEPER

When I explain the five levels of trance, my clients immediately want to challenge the idea that all levels of trance are equally valid. (They suspect it is the sex therapy equivalent of "everybody should have prizes.") After all, who wants to settle for casual or routine? My first defense is that it is impossible to reach the deeper layers without going through the first two. Second, the lower levels of trance can be a platform for launching into another type of lovemaking.

If you have been following the program thus far, the Month of Sensuality will have already introduced you to some of the pleasures of trance. This chapter's exercise section, "Progressive Relaxation," will also help you progress to a deeper level.

Otherwise, my advice is to take it slow and allow plenty of time. The key is to get the ambiance right and use lots of repetitive strokes (occasionally changing direction, pressure, and area of skin covered). If any images float into your mind, focus on them and try to brighten the colors; imagine what is around the corner and heighten the overall experience. Concentrate on all the sensations of lovemaking, so touch becomes a caress, not a tickle. Heavy breathing becomes sensuous (and a sign of just how turned on your partner has become). Smells and tastes become appetizing and animalistic rather than disgusting. Finally, the naked body is not embarrassing but vulnerable and erotic.

## Creative Play

In this kind of lovemaking, sex is an adventure. The mood is playful, fun, and dramatic. Mosher called this "role play," but I find this term narrow because these lovers use a whole range of practices to keep their sex life vital and adventurous. While, for many couples, fantasy is something only whispered (or more probably kept private), creative couples share and act out their desires together. In trance, the emphasis is on repetitive patterns and soothing movements, whereas in creative lovemaking, it is on variety (especially of techniques, positions, props, and toys). Common role plays include teacher and naughty school boy or girl, doctors and nurses, prison guard and prisoner, prostitute and customer, jockey and pony, and sultan in the harem. The possibilities are endless, but many have an element of power, although it is not always obvious who is in control.

Jack, forty-two, is gay and likes to spice up his love life by occasionally playing a game. "My partner and I are the groom and best man sharing the same bed on the night before the wedding. Whether it is too much to drink, last-minute nerves, or just overwhelming desire, one of us will 'seduce' the other. He will pretend not to be 'like that' and ask coyly, 'Why are you touching me there?' but it doesn't take long before the groom relents and we make passionate love. Sometimes I like to pretend I'm straight or sometimes to be the 'gay' best friend coming out about his secret desires, but any way around, the drama is always very satisfying."

Creative people feel good enough about themselves to step out of their everyday identity and adopt a different sexual persona. Some couples only talk about their fantasies, for example, being discovered making love somewhere public, while others will act them out (and take a blanket into a secluded park). Many couples dress up to truly get into the role and have props to set the mood (for example, a lump of sugar for the pony) or use toys to provide variety in their lovemaking.

A peak sexual experience is when instead of playing a role, each partner becomes the role. This is eyes-open, lights-on lovemaking. Talking is important for pulling each other deeper into the fantasy or as part of assuming another character. These couples are the ones least likely to restrict their lovemaking to the bedroom.

The worst outcome for lovers of creative play is when a partner just goes through the motions or reminds them of who they really are. Other dislikes include mediocre, lackluster, and repetitive sex or when one partner drifts off into a private world before the fantasy has had time to breathe and establish itself. Creative lovers accept that their partner is not an actor but hate holding back, rating skills, or allowing an internal critical voice to take hold. Laughter is fine, because this kind of sex is joyful. Laughter *at* someone's desires or how they choose to express them, however, is never acceptable.

### Levels of Creative Play

Once again there are five levels, and each person has to find the level at which he or she feels comfortable. To progress deeper into role play does not necessarily mean complicated props, a kinky imagination, or a lack of inhibitions, but the desire to throw yourself into and enjoy the game.

- *Casual:* At the most basic level, when you cannot or feel unable to explain the fantasy to your partner, this is a private experience. Unfortunately, this means no props, sexy talk, or opportunity to deepen and develop the scenario. Common casual role plays, where the partner is excluded, include imagining making love to a celebrity or an acquaintance. With minimal cooperation (wearing sexy lingerie), there is still a complete cut-off between the character (sensual woman) and the real self (bored and doing it to keep the peace).

- *Routine:* Both partners are clearly aware of the game, but one or both are going through the motions or imagining the character in a nonsexual role. Another example of routine role play is when fantasies are overused and become stale and predictable. Alternatively, the roles are unfocused and traditional, as if the couple are "playing" dutiful husband and wife, rather than accepting each other in all their contradictory complexity.

- *Engrossed:* Instead of playing a role, you *become* the role and stop worrying about what each other thinks or whether you're doing it "right" and just enjoy yourselves. All the cares of the day are thrown off, and there is a childish sense of play and wonder.

- *Entranced:* The action flows without either of you thinking about or directing the scenario. It is like you can communicate without words—facial expressions, sounds, and movement are enough—as you push each other to the heights of passion. When an orgasm comes, it is dramatic, lusty, and often takes you by surprise.

- *Ecstatic:* There is such a fit between the role and you that it reveals something deep about yourself, or you learn something new about your partner. For example, Jack grew up in homophobic community, and his groom fantasy allowed him to challenge the idea that everybody was heterosexual. Fully formed role play can also be healing too, as "coming out" to the groom allowed Jack to put the pain of rejection (by some of his real friends) into a sexual game where he is always accepted and rewarded.

## HOW TO GO DEEPER

Although pretending to make love to someone other than your partner can provide an orgasm and be a pleasant break from everyday life, it is not a long-term answer to a disappointing sex life. There can also be comfort through routine lovemaking in long-established roles, but it is easy for one partner to get bored, and, in the worst-case scenario, be tempted to have an affair. However, there can be much resistance to going deeper.

Jack's partner, Sean, had been cautious about playing Jack's games. "Where is it going to end? That's what I want to know. Are you going to want me to tie you up and beat you?" This is a common misconception, and Jack was able to reassure him that he had no interest in sadomasochism.

The best creative play either has a strong match with who you are or offers a vacation from your everyday life, including the beliefs handed down by your parents, teachers, church, etc. For example, if you believe that "nice women do not solicit sex," it can be liberating to play a "bad" girl on the prowl. If you believe that "a man should give women orgasms," it is a relief to play a helpless virgin to a Mrs. Robinson. In my experience, you have to reach a certain level of maturity to fully embrace the joys of role play. It takes time to grow into yourself and even more time to find enough self-belief to be able to play with this hard-won identity without losing touch with the real you.

Set aside plenty of time to talk with your partner about your desires and fears about creative play. The exercises in Chapter One should have improved your overall communication. So hear each other out, ask questions, and be sure you've heard each other correctly before dismissing any ideas. Maybe with a few changes, you could enter into your partner's imaginary world.

So what holds you back? It is a fear of failure or not being good enough. Having worked with actors (on the plays I've written) and been trained to "role play" clients with relationship problems, I have two pieces of advice: Don't block and don't wimp out. Blocking is where someone says, "We're on the moon," and you reply, "No we're not. I can see the supermarket parking lot." Instead, you could reply, "That's why we're floating" or "It's so beautiful."

Wimping out is when you say, "I can't do this," or "I'm not creative." Instead of blocking or wimping out, try silencing your inner critic and going with the flow for a while. Remember, what counts to creative lovers is not the skill but how much you enter into the spirit of the game.

The other fear that impedes experimentation with creative play is a concern that *all* sex will have to involve games, props, or something kinky. Please let me reassure you: I've yet to take a couple through this part of the program and met someone who *only* wants creative sex. These people value variety and therefore embrace the other two styles of lovemaking, as long as their desires are taken into consideration from time to time.

## Partner-Focused

For these people, making love is not the isolation tank of trance or the theatrical props and setting of creative play. The focus is on their relationship and how they feel about the other. There is affectionate sweet talk and intimate conversations before, during, and after sex. These couples enjoy valentines, love songs, romance, and closeness. The style is eyes open, lots of kissing, cuddling, and full-body contact. No wonder they consider sex to be a loving merger.

Rick is forty and has been married to Elaine for ten years. "I really like the deep connection of lovemaking, watching the pleasure across her face as I enter, and hearing her sharp intake of breath. I love teasing her by slowing down when she wants to go faster, so she has to beg for release. Afterward, we cuddle, and I feel rejuvenated and ready for anything."

Anything that deepens a loving bond and helps "really know someone" is always popular with partner-focused lovers. They read romantic novels and enjoy "sappy" films. Foreplay is incredibly important to help get in the mood. Although lovemaking is normally in the bedroom, they also like a "romantic" setting like a four-poster bed or a log fire. These are sensual people who enjoy satin sheets, lingering touch, and open-mouth kissing. Traditionally, this style has been considered the woman's choice, but I have plenty of male clients who prefer this kind of love-making.

For partner-focused lovers, it is disconcerting when their lover is going through the motions or is not present, especially if, like Rick, giving pleasure to their partner gives them pleasure. Partner-focused lovers are often reticent to role play and can take it as a form of criticism ("Why aren't I good enough?") or feel their "special connection" will be challenged or changed as a result of dressing up or introducing props or toys.

### Levels of Partner-Focused Sex

The depth of partner-focused lovemaking depends on the quality of the bond between the lovers. At the lower levels, it could be a one-night stand or causal ongoing sex, but to achieve a deeper depth, long-term commitment is necessary. However, it is not just the nature of the relationship that affects this kind of lovemaking but the emotional maturity of each partner.

- *Casual:* At this level, the other person is a means to an orgasmic end or sometimes to satisfy needs that are not necessarily sexual, such as revenge, money, power, or social status. In effect, there is no real engagement with the partner beyond needs, pleasure, and orgasm.

- *Routine:* At this level, the other person is a source of comfort, and the closeness and physical pleasure help you feel better after a hard day in a cruel world. This is generally tenderer than casual partner-focused sex, but the partner can be a prop for private fantasy (either standing in for a celebrity or colleague at work, or imagining something exhibitionist/ forbidden) rather than being invited to share in the fantasy. Ultimately, if the other partner enjoys the sex, it's a bonus rather than a focus.

- *Engrossed:* This is the first level where each partner's pleasure is equally important. The partner is a mirror, and the compliments and sweet talk bolster your ego and make you feel good about yourself. Through his or her eyes, you are beautiful—even if you don't quite believe it yourself. There is focus on surface qualities, and you admire your partner's physical attributes and his or her skills as a lover. Although you do not necessarily want your own and your partner's fantasies to match—or more likely feel unable to share yours, or are frightened to ask about his or hers—you are a considerate lover, keen to match and pace mounting levels of excitement. Mosher described this kind of lovemaking: "Sex is a duo sonata, and not a concerto, in which the genitals are the lead instruments."

- *Entranced:* Your partner is a real person. Finally, you can take off your mask and be who you truly are, and your partner can do the same. There is an acceptance about each other's weaknesses as well as strengths, until even blemishes and imperfections are beautiful. This is lovemaking with eyes open and lights on. The fantasies are shared, romantic, poetic expressions of your love for each other.

- *Ecstatic:* At this level, the other person enters a spiritual dimension. Lovemaking is a mystic union between yourself and your partner. The boundaries between the two of you have dissolved into a loving merger where "now and then" and "here and there" are transcended. This is the world of Tantric sex where orgasms are often irrelevant.

## HOW TO GO DEEPER

Although casual and routine partner-focused lovemaking does not sound particularly appetizing (especially if a lot of your sex fits this category), there is still a place for it in a well-rounded relationship. However much you love each other, there will be times when you argue and have "angry" sex together. Sometimes greedy lovemaking can be a turn on for both parties. Equally, there are occasions when comfort sex is just what the doctor ordered.

I sometimes meet couples who want their lovemaking to *always* be entranced, and although there is nothing wrong with this goal, it can ruin your sex life. These couples are deeply in love and care too much for each other's pleasures—to the point that they are sexually constipated. To achieve this level of union, they need plenty of free time and to be purged from the stresses of everyday life. The result is that they seldom make love.

Having made those provisos, how do you go deeper? The answer will probably be a shock: argue more. We live in a society that is uncomfortable with anger and confrontation. However, they bring buried issues up to the surface and create a sense that something must be done. It might be nicer to turn the other cheek and pretend something does not matter, but it is not honest. Remember, the deeper levels of partner-focused sex involve taking the mask off and trusting that your partner will accept all of you—not just the "nice" bits. Ultimately, having an argument with your partner is one of the most intimate things you can do, because it shows you care enough to engage rather than pretend everything's okay.

# INCOMPATIBLE SEX STYLES

When I explain the three styles of lovemaking to clients, some couples worry that unless they agree on their preferred style that their relationship is doomed. However, I am quick to reassure that ultimately it does not matter.

First, there is plenty of overlap between the different styles (particularly at the deeper levels). For example, deep trance can become very partner-focused, and creative play sometimes reveals more about you than partner-focused sex (because it can bring the painful, difficult, or rough edges of your personality to the fore). Second, a range of enjoyed styles of lovemaking, instead of just sticking to one, can help sustain passion and interest in your sex life.

## ADDING FLAIR

Light bondage (hands tied with a silk scarf) can provide the stimulation for creative play while the slight restriction can heighten the pleasures of the trance. Similarly, light spanking (hardly more than a pat or a tap) can feed the patterned play for trance and the power fantasies often attached to creative play.

## Trance and Creative Play

When I explored the three styles of lovemaking with Janine and Greg, whom we met earlier in this chapter, it became clear that while she enjoyed trance, he liked the idea of creative play. So I sent them away to experiment. They returned the next week all smiles, but it turned out that things hadn't gone quite to plan.

"When Janine goes off into her trance, she often finds herself by water or the sea, carried away by the power of huge wave. As she was reading a book about Vikings, I suggested that we pretend." Greg paused, embarrassed.

"What's the matter?" I asked.

"It's personal."

"That's the beauty of fantasy; it reveals so much about you."

Greg took a deep breath. "So we pretended that I was a marauding Viking who'd ransacked the village and had taken Janine back to my boat to be raped and pillaged."

"We had a wonderful time and a real connection, honestly," said Janine.

"But when we were kissing and cuddling afterward, Janine explained that Viking longboats didn't have masts, as I had mentioned in my sexy talk. I'd somehow crossed over into *Pirates of the Caribbean,* and she was tied to the rigging and forced to walk the plank unless she submitted to my evil plans. For a second, I was upset because I'd put a lot of effort into the story, but then we laughed and had another cuddle."

*How can trance and creative play couples complement each other?* The creative partner needs to keep the "script" as simple as possible so that it does not intrude too much on the unstructured fantasies of the trance partner. Meanwhile, the trance partner needs to be aware that creative lovers enjoy a variety of settings for sex and often enjoy dressing up. As Greg had tried to enter her world, Janine decided to return the favor. The next week, she arranged for the children to stay over at their grandparents and brought the duvet in front of the open fire in the living room and circled it with candles. (This fulfilled her need for privacy, security, and sensuality.) She also put on a lacy garter and suspenders and some of her best jewelry.

"I was completely thrilled," said Greg, "partly because she'd been to all this trouble, but mainly because she looked so beautiful by candlelight."

It also inspired a fantasy for Greg where he was a highway man who had been seduced by a lady so he would let her keep her jewels. Remembering how intrusive Janine had found the details last time, he kept the lusty talk to a minimum. The evening had been a complete success and helped them find a compromise for the future where Greg had variety and Janine had the rhythmic foreplay that allowed her to slip deeper into the sensual pleasures of lovemaking.

## Trance and Partner-Focused

In the case of Rick and Elaine, whom we met earlier, the main source of conflict was that Rick felt Elaine would slip off into her own private world of trance leaving Rick feeling marooned.

"Sometimes, it can feel very lonely making love to Elaine because I feel she's not really there," explained Rick.

"But I'm just enjoying myself, until he keeps asking me to open my eyes to look at him," Elaine said.

Once they understood that theirs was quite a common dilemma, and that there was no right or wrong way to make love, the heat was taken out of their fights. It was time to find middle ground.

*How can trance and partner-focused couples complement each other?* With these couples, I try to lengthen the amount of foreplay. In this way, the first ten or fifteen minutes of lovemaking can be dedicated to kissing, eye contact, and loving endearments, which are so important to partner-focused lovers but can be intrusive when someone is deep into trance. This allowed Rick to feel a strong enough connection with Elaine so that he did not feel abandoned as their lovemaking progressed.

My next task was to help Elaine give some feedback to Rick because I suspected that he thought Elaine's silence was an indication of her disinterest in their lovemaking.

"Do you feel turned on?" I asked Elaine.

"Of course," she responded. "But I keep quiet because I don't want to wake the children."

I encouraged Rick and Elaine to use background music to mask any sounds while they made love and allow Elaine to "give voice" to her inner-feelings, not in a *When Harry Met Sally* fake way, but to vocalize what was inside. This strategy was a great success.

"Being able to let go and moan and sigh allowed me to fall deeper into all the lovely sensations," explained Elaine.

"Not only did I enjoy her reactions, which were really wonderful, but I became more aware of other signs of her enjoyment, like heavy breathing," said Rick.

## ADDING FLAIR

Put extra emphasis on after-play. Kissing and cuddling after orgasm as a form of pillow talk and offering a few good reviews are important to partner-focused lovers. This was particularly effective when Elaine gave Rick positive feedback on the images he helped her create in her trance.

### Partner-Focused and Creative Play

This combination has the most potential for conflict. With partner-focused lovemaking, the relationship is center stage and anything else is seen as either a distraction, or worse, not just undermining the sex act but threatening the whole relationship. During counseling, Sean, the partner of Jack who enjoyed the wedding-night role play, found the courage to say something that had been troubling him:

"It's like I'm not enough for him. I worry that he'll start stop playing and actually start seducing straight men."

"What would that be like?" I asked.

"Devastating. I don't know if I could cope with the rejection."

Jack wanted to interrupt and tell him it was only a fantasy, but I stopped him. It is important to allow your partner to give full voice to his or her fears.

"What does 'devastating' mean?" I asked Sean. "You'd turn into a quivering piece of jelly that barely functions?"

"No. Of course, I'd be able to function, go to work, that sort of thing."

Once Sean had confronted the reality of his fears and the fact that something horrible would not destroy him, he was able to listen to Jack's reassurance.

"I'm not interested in straight men. What would we have in common? I love you."

Although the peace had been restored, I was aware that Jack had fears as well. People who enjoy role play want variety (different positions, techniques, and places to make love) and tend to become easily bored by the same eyes-open, face-to-face routine that is a central part of partner-focused lovemaking. So how would Jack feel if there was no opportunity for fantasy and role play?

"Everything would be vanilla," Jack admitted.

I asked him to elaborate.

"There're hundreds of flavors of ice cream and I might not like them all, but I don't think I want to return to the world of my childhood where there was only vanilla or strawberry, if you were lucky."

Sean wanted to reassure him, but I stopped him.

"What would strictly vanilla sex be like?" I inquired.

"Dull, boring, routine, going through the motions."

"What would that be like? You'd get fed up and stop having sex?"

"I'd never get *that* bored."

Once both of their fears were out in the open, and not as overwhelming as each first thought, they were both ready to find a way forward.

*How can partner-focused and creative play couples complement each other?* If you're partner-focused, concentrate on how much role play reveals about your partner. In this way, you can reframe the experience into something intimate that deepens your understanding of each other. If you enjoy creative play, be aware that your partner will feel most comfortable in a role that is closest to his or her own identity or does not challenge his or her sense of identity.

## ADDING FLAIR

There are lots of ways to fulfill creative lovers' needs for variety while helping partner-focused partners feel valued and secure. These include making love in places other than the bedroom, experimenting with different techniques, and food play. Smearing each other with yogurt, running a piece of ice over each other's skin on a hot night, or eating fruit off each other's bodies and passing it back and forth with passionate kisses are enjoyable in both styles of lovemaking. Finally, be grateful that although you and your partner have different ideas about sex, the issues are out in the open and can be discussed.

## DESTRUCTIVE SCENARIOS

To help my clients get in touch with their preferred styles of lovemaking, I take them through a questionnaire (see the exercise section). When I ask certain questions, I can almost feel the pressure in the room for each partner to come up with the same answer. I've even made couples do the test back to back so there are no "meaningful" looks exchanged. I accept it can be distressing or even disturbing to discover your partner is not your twin, especially when it comes to sex, but it is better than a forced match. Time and again, I discover couples doing not what they want but what has *not* been ruled out. If this sounds familiar, how do you get around the problem?

When it comes to experimenting with sex, we have a deep-rooted fear of stepping off the primrose path. Popular stories from Adam and Eve to Little Red Riding Hood tell us that one mistake will get us thrown out of the Garden of Eden or gobbled up by a hungry wolf. Yet wouldn't it be thrilling to dance with the wolves, and maybe, just maybe, you'd like to be a wolf yourself? Except you'll never know how far into the woods you'd like to stray until you have the courage to embark on your own journey of discovery. Remember, you are only *experimenting*, not signing a contract binding you forever to pursue this style of lovemaking.

> *"When it comes to experimenting with sex,*
> *we have a deep-rooted fear of stepping off the primrose path."*

Game Theory, the study of cooperation and the underlying strategies that shape human behavior, offers insight into the other two patterns that undermine passionate and plentiful lovemaking. The first of these is called "Chicken" after the scene in *Rebel without a Cause* where James Dean and his rival race stolen cars toward an abyss. The loser is the first person to jump out. Chicken explains how the world got to the edge of a nuclear war over the Cuban Missile Crisis (with the Russians refusing to remove their missiles and the Americans refusing to remove their blockade). However, this "game" is best illustrated, for our purposes, by the classic dilemma of two strangers walking toward each other down a narrow street. For each person, the positive outcome is when the other steps into the gutter. The worst outcome is if neither backs down and they are stuck in the narrow street. There is, of course, a neutral outcome where both parties step aside.

When I look into the sex life of many couples, I find they are playing a version of Chicken in which each partner wants a different kind of love-making (typically the scenario includes one partner-focused and one role-play partner). All too often they are trapped by brinkmanship, which leaves each partner on opposite sides of the bed until one partner backs down. Normally, this puts the partner least interested in sex in the driver's seat as he or she can always "win" a war by putting off sex, waiting to be "sweet talked," or offering sex as a reward. There is a different version where the most-interested partner effectively blackmails the other into stepping up lovemaking. For example, an affair has happened and the betrayed partner is fearful of losing the partner again, so he or she will do whatever it takes, even if it isn't the typical style. Although this might create a positive outcome for one party, it undermines the long-term health of the relationship, and everybody loses.

The other game is called "Battle of the Sexes." The classic scenario is one person wants to go the movies but the other wants to go to a sporting event. In some ways, this game is like Chicken. However, this time around, we are dealing with a couple who would prefer the other to come with them, rather than attend their activity alone. In what game theorists call the "perfect" version of the game, the couple discusses the alternatives. (In the "imperfect" version, there is no discussion and each person hopes the other will acquiesce.)

In his book about game theory, *Rock, Paper, Scissors* (Hay House, 2008), Len Fisher gives a personal example of this dilemma. Len is Australian and his wife is British, so they divide their time equally between the two countries and enjoy two summers. However, Len prefers to be in Australia and his wife, Wendy, prefers the UK so each would ask the other for longer time on home turf. Many couples face this Battle of the Sexes dilemma with their lovemaking. Both partners are happy to go along with the other's preferred type of sex, so the choice is between two reasonable outcomes, but they would still rather have their own way. If this sounds familiar, how do you break any potential deadlock? Hopefully, in your relationship, you can discuss sex, so it is a "perfect" rather than an "imperfect" version of the game.

The Fishers tried to do a cost-benefit analysis of their dilemma and decided Len would go to Australia a little earlier and stay for a while after Wendy returned to the UK. He got a lot of work done, but he didn't enjoy the time apart. Meanwhile, Wendy had to close their UK home on her own. So Len decided to resolve their problem by adopting the strategy of Israeli-American game theorist Robert Aumann, who won the 2005 Nobel Prize for Economics for his understanding of cooperation and conflict. His solution for Battle of the Sexes is simple: both parties agree to a random way of determining the outcome, for example, cutting cards, flipping a coin, or playing "rock, paper, scissors."

So the Fishers' annual dilemma is resolved by tossing a coin. If it's heads, Len stays in England and comes to Australia at the same time as his wife. If it's tails, Wendy comes to Australia earlier with Len.

However, there is another way forward and one which draws on the neutral outcome of Chicken (where both parties step aside). I call this "Giving and Receiving."

## GIVING AND RECEIVING

Many couples get stuck in very strict roles. Traditionally the man will "do" the woman, i.e., give pleasure and drive his lover to the heights of an orgasm. Similarly with gay and lesbian couples, one partner will have the active role and take charge of the lovemaking. However, the "giving" partner can find it hard to let go and receive pleasure. By contrast, someone who is "done" will enjoy the surrender of lovemaking and is happy to receive. Unfortunately, this partner does not experience the pleasure of giving or have the opportunity to harness the full power of her, or occasionally his, sexuality.

One of the best ways of sustaining good lovemaking is learning the power of swapping "doing" and "being done." It also helps circumnavigate the problems of forced matches, Chicken, or Battle of the Sexes as lovemaking becomes a partnership with an outcome where both partners win.

## Giving

Giving involves:

- Generosity
- Initiating or proposing sex
- Taking the lead on what happens during sex
- Setting the pace
- Seduction
- Tasting
- Moving into your partner (or if a woman is in this role, moving herself onto her partner's penis, tongue, or fingers)
- Sending your partner over the edge
- Focusing on his or her responses
- Enjoying his or her moans and sighs and getting pleasure from his or her pleasure (as much as your own)
- Power

## Receiving

Receiving involves:

- Allowing yourself to be seduced
- Surrender: "Take me, I'm yours."
- Total absorption in the ecstasy of the moment
- Freedom from everyday life and concerns
- Devotion
- Opening up. For a woman, this means letting your partner enter you with his penis, tongue, or fingers. For a man, this can involve the woman being on top and setting the pace for intercourse by raising

herself up and down or tensing and relaxing her vaginal muscles. With oral sex, it means letting her lick and tease your penis rather than thrusting it into her mouth. For gay men, receiving includes anal intercourse. Incidentally, many heterosexual men enjoy their partner inserting her finger into his anus and massaging his prostate gland.

## LETTING GO

It takes a certain amount of confidence to enjoy both roles of giver and receiver. Unfortunately, some men find it hard to let go and "be done." As one sex therapist remarked, "Some men use sex to screw their penis on tighter." Everybody laughed, partly because it was such a graphic way of explaining men's fears that giving up control of sex will somehow unman them, but mainly because we recognized the fear in our clients, or maybe in ourselves. Similarly, some women find it difficult to let themselves go completely, fearing it will be unladylike. Others are embarrassed to show their full potency and womanly potential (often for fear of hurting their partner's ego). Ultimately, both men and women are frightened of their sexual power and of truly controlling or truly surrendering to the pleasures of lovemaking.

Once you have completed the Two Weeks of Variety and begin to expand your range of sexual destinations, it is time not only to reintroduce intercourse (if you haven't already) but also to discuss who initiates sex in your relationship.

- Who is most likely to take charge and either suggest sex or start the seduction process?

- Talk to each other about what it is like to be in charge. What are the advantages? What are the disadvantages? (For example, risk of rejection.) Is it always clear when the person initiating is asking for sex and when he or she is asking for another form of being intimate?

- If you are the person in charge of initiating (most of the time), what would it be like to give up control and wait to be asked? How would your partner make his or her desires clear? What are the fears about waiting for your partner to initiate? How long do you think you might have to wait?

- If you are the person who normally waits to be seduced, what would it be like to initiate, express your desire, or ask for sex? What are your fears? What is exciting about the prospect?

- Make a contract and swap roles. If it is you who is waiting to be asked, there should be no hints, comments, or anything else that suggests impatience or pressure (even jokes count). Remember, this is total surrender.

- Are there other ways that the person in charge of initiating could retain control during lovemaking too? What changes would allow each of you to fully experience the pleasures of giving and receiving?

- Afterward, look back and evaluate. What have you learned? Did the person who normally initiates have to wait as long as he or she expected, or just a few days longer than usual? Did he or she feel truly desired for once? Did the person who usually waits to be asked feel empowered and in charge of his or her sexuality?

## SOMETHING TO SLEEP ON

In summary, remember:

- Sex becomes boring (and inauthentic) when we are frightened to let our partner see our full complexity.

- There are three styles of lovemaking. In trance, sex is like meditation and focused on inner pleasures. In creative play, sex is dramatic and as varied as the mood and the fantasy create. In partner-focused lovemaking, sex is about union, and an orgasm will be the most intense when the couple feel closest.

- With each type, there are five levels of intensity. At the basic levels, sex can happen with almost anyone—as long as they have the necessary skills. However, it takes a loving and committed relationship to achieve the full intensity of each type of sex.

- There is often an overlap of sex styles and mediating them is necessary for pleasurable sex.

- Enjoying both receiving and giving allows couples to go deeper into the three styles of lovemaking to the place where being partner-focused, trance, and creative play overlap and intertwine. Lovemaking is no longer about game playing or winning or losing but about cooperation.

# SEX ED

## EXERCISE 15    PROGRESSIVE RELAXATION

Anxiety inhibits good sex, but feeling relaxed promotes it. The following exercise will help you achieve the right frame of mind, especially if engaging in a style of lovemaking that is not typical for you.

1. **Set aside time to relax.** Ideally, you should lie down on a flat surface. However, progressive relaxation can be slotted into idle moments at work or commuting. In these situations, do the exercise sitting down with your feet firmly on the ground.

2. **Attend to your breathing.** Put your hands over your rib cage and feel your lungs expanding and contracting. Allow your breathing to deepen, and imagine that every time you exhale, all the stress flows out of your body.

3. **Progressively tense and relax each of your muscle groups.** Start with your toes, tense for ten seconds, release and repeat. Next move on to your knees, then buttocks, then stomach, shoulders, arms, neck, jaw, eyes, and forehead. Pause between each muscle group, take a deep breath, and let it out with a sigh.

4. **Allow your body to go limp.** Make certain every muscle in your body is as relaxed as possible and then return to part two of the exercise and go through parts three and four a couple of times.

## EXERCISE 16    TEST YOUR SEXUAL STYLE

For many people, there is a difference between their preferred style of lovemaking and what they and their partner normally do. To help you discover your true sexual style and whether it matches your partner's, I have adapted the following questionnaire from Mosher's original "Sexual Path Preferences Inventory."

Look through the following statements and choose the options that best match your opinions about making love. Don't take too long on this exercise; go with the first idea that pops into your head, and remember there are no right or wrong answers. Think what you would *truly* enjoy the most, not what you *should* answer.

1. When it comes to the right ambiance for lovemaking, I prefer:

   a. Sex in a romantic context where my partner and I are feeling loving toward each other.

   b. Sex in a setting close to nature—for example, a field of long grass or on a beach—assuming we were totally alone and could be sure of not being disturbed.

   c. Sex in a dramatic setting—for example, a New Orleans brothel, a harem, or a medieval dungeon.

2. When it comes to intercourse technique, I prefer:

   a. Face to face with the one I love.

   b. A wide variety of positions.

   c. Slow and rhythmic movements, which allow me to enjoy the shades of pleasure during intercourse.

3. My ideal sex is:

   a. A drama that begins with attraction, develops a plot filled with intrigue, mystery, and sex play, and ends with a tumultuous orgasm.

   b. A trip into a world of sensory images and tingling nerve endings.

   c. An expression of love for my partner.

4. I'm most likely to be in the mood for passionate sex when:

   a. I'm physically relaxed and mentally receptive.

   b. I'm feeling really loving toward my partner.

   c. I'm feeling playful and adventurous.

5. When it comes to the perfect place for making love, I would choose:

   a. A semipublic place to make secret love.

   b. Somewhere that ensures total privacy.

   c. Somewhere that has special meaning for me and my partner.

6. When it comes to foreplay, my first choice would be:

   a. Kissing the face and the lips and the neck.

   b. Plenty of accomplished oral sex.

   c. Anything where the pacing and repetition permits us to become absorbed into the moment.

7. In an ideal world, my sex partner would have:

   a. A flair for experimenting and good technique.

   b. The ability to flow with my mood rather than trying to dictate how sex is done.

   c. Lots of love to give.

8. The type of pillow talk that I prefer is:

   a. Moans and sighs or something like "That feels good."

   b. Compliments, and, best of all, "I love you."

   c. Urging, begging, or directing, "Harder, take me, more, more, yes."

9. When it comes to fantasies, I'm most likely to enjoy:

   a. The idea that my partner is pledging his or her love and devotion through sex.

   b. The novelty of imagining different activities, settings, and people.

   c. Using my imagination to sink further into the sensual experience.

10. If I had to choose my favorite recipe for good sex, it would be:

   a. A wide variety of sex practices and positions for intercourse.

   b. The love we feel for each other.

   c. Intense involvement in the sexual and sensual sensation of the moment.

11. If I was going to play music during sex, I would choose something:

   a. Soft and low that facilitates the mood without setting a pace to be followed.

   b. Lyrical, romantic, and poetic to match my partner's loving mood.

   c. Dramatic and exciting rhythms that frame and feed my fantasies.

12. Pick the statement with which you most strongly agree:

    a. An ideal sex partner knows exactly what I like and want.

    b. I enjoy a partner who is open to playing different roles so we can keep our lovemaking varied and exciting.

    c. If my partner cannot look me in the eye before, during, and after sex, I suspect the attraction is to the act of sex and not to me.

13. Pick the emotion you most associate with sex:

    a. Love.

    b. Excitement.

    c. Enjoyment.

14. For me sex is:

    a. The merging of two into one.

    b. Setting aside the pressures of daily life and being transported into a world of pleasure.

    c. A cathartic drama that helps me process and cope with the demands made on me in the real world.

15. For me the best orgasm is:

    a. A moment of total surrender to intense pleasures.

    b. An overwhelming dramatic shock that releases my sexual tension.

    c. A unique moment of fusion when my soul cries out its love and my longing for my partner is fulfilled.

## Results

| | | | |
|---|---|---|---|
| 1. | a. Partner-Focused | b. Trance | c. Creative Play |
| 2. | a. Partner-Focused | b. Creative Play | c. Trance |
| 3. | a. Creative Play | b. Trance | c. Partner-Focused |
| 4. | a. Trance | b. Partner-Focused | c. Creative Play |
| 5. | a. Creative Play | b. Trance | c. Partner-Focused |
| 6. | a. Partner-Focused | b. Creative Play | c. Trance |
| 7. | a. Creative Play | b. Trance | c. Partner-Focused |
| 8. | a. Trance | b. Partner-Focused | c. Creative Play |
| 9. | a. Partner-Focused | b. Creative Play | c. Trance |
| 10. | a. Creative Play | b. Partner-Focused | c. Trance |
| 11. | a. Trance | b. Partner-Focused | c. Creative Play |
| 12. | a. Trance | b. Creative Play | c. Partner-Focused |
| 13. | a. Partner-Focused | b. Creative Play | c. Trance |
| 14. | a. Partner-Focused | b. Trance | c. Creative Play |
| 15. | a. Trance | b. Creative Play | c. Partner-Focused |

## How to interpret your results:

- Total up the number of responses for each type of lovemaking. Most people will have a preferred and secondary type. Although, periodically, I come across people who are versatile and spread across all three.

- Discuss with your partner what you have discovered about your preferred style and what surprised you.

- Concentrate on the similarities between you and your partner. Where do you match? Is there an overlap between first and second preferences?

- Compare your current couple lovemaking style with your preferences. What ingredients could you include, from time to time, to enhance and deepen your sexual repertoire?

- What's stopping you from enjoying your preferred type? Don't just blame your partner but look at your upbringings and the messages you were given about sex. What would help you shed these restrictions and embrace your true sexuality?

# Chapter Seven

# Set Free Your Fantasy

Sexuality is a powerful window into who you are, and that includes what you desire and fantasize about. Unfortunately, many people are frightened to take a long honest look at their fantasies, partly because they worry about not liking what they might find and partly because they fear that their partner might not find this version of themselves acceptable. So they fall into one of two traps: cover their eyes and peep through their fingers at their own sexuality or squelch their natural curiosity about their sexuality by using secondhand fantasies from pornographers. Women are likelier to fall into the first trap and men, the second.

However, fantasies are universal and part of what makes humans human. So the goal of this chapter is to remove some of the fear, understand the purpose fantasies serve, and explain how to harness them to improve lovemaking.

Brett Kahr is a senior clinical research fellow at the Winnicott Clinic in Surrey, England, and has gathered the sexual fantasies of eighteen thousand adults who either filled out an Internet questionnaire or had a face-to-face interview. The results of this research, which was limited to England, are published in *Sex and the Psyche* (Penguin, 2007). Kahr believes that virtually all men and women have private sexual fantasies. In his Internet research, 96 percent of men and 84 percent of women reported that they fantasized, but the number increased when he conducted private interviews. In fact, Kahr met only a handful of women who insisted that they did not fantasize, but after a five-hour interview, they disclosed their sexual fantasies.

There are two types of fantasy. The first is the type we reveal to our friends or partners. These will often feature celebrities, are generally "clean," and reveal little or nothing about us. The second level is shared with great reluctance (possibly only to a researcher or anonymously in an Internet chat room). In sharp contrast to our public fantasies, these are detailed, "dirty," and sometimes disturbing.

## THE TOP FIVE UNDISCLOSED FANTASIES

1. Playing a dominant or aggressive role during sex—33 percent
2. Playing a submissive or passive role during sex—29 percent
3. Being tied up by someone—25 percent
4. Tying someone up—23 percent
5. Blindfolding someone else—17 percent

## THE FANTASY SPECTRUM

Although in reality our sex lives can be disappointing and dull, in our imaginations we are always desired, uninhibited, and unconstrained. So it is no surprise that the respondents to Kahr's survey came up with thousands of different fantasies. Some of the scenarios were simple (just a few images and one partner), while others were complex (with involved plots and a large cast). Quite a few involved powerful presidents, historical and religious figures, and even the Queen of England! At first sight, this seemed like the strangest discovery; however, these fantasies represent childhood, religion, and authority, which are predominant in most people's formative years, so on second thought, these finding were understandable. To give a clearer picture of our fantasies, I have organized them into ten categories with some overlap.

### Partners

According to Kahr, a significant proportion of the people fantasize about their regular partner during sex: 10 percent every time; 16 percent very often. However, there is quite a difference between how younger people, who have not been with their partner as long, and those age fifty and older responded. With those eighteen to twenty-nine, 14 percent fantasize about their partner every time, but people over fifty reported 6 percent. These fantasies include "having stamina to make love in every room in the house (up to fifteen rooms) in a continuous session" and "sex with my husband just like it was before we got married." In my research, I found many people fantasize about their first time with their partner.

"I remember that look on her face as I was poised to enter her, full of lust and abandon, such a sexy combination," said Scott, forty-seven. "I pushed her legs further back, so she was completely exposed. I teased the entrance with my tip, and she moaned. I gave her this look that said 'you want it,' she tried to tilt upward to capture me, but I shook my head. This would be on my terms, and at that moment, she smiled and we melted into one another. That was over fifteen years ago, and I still get excited thinking about it."

Another popular partner fantasy is making love in romantic places.

"We're on this beach at midnight. It's warm and tropical, and we can hear the cicadas in the bushes as we walk down the cliff path to the sea," said Sophie, twenty-eight. "My husband takes my hands and swings me around, faster and faster, until we fall together laughing in a heap on the sand. We start kissing, and it gets more and more passionate and urgent. The tide is coming in. I can taste the saltwater on his lips, and I'm feeling hot inside, but the cooling waves are lapping over my naked feet. He pulls me up the beach and pulls my clothes off at the same time. In the moonlight, I have this perfect body and he kisses me all over. I come without him touching me down there."

## People Other Than Partners

Although our partners would like to believe that we are thinking of them while making love, this not necessarily the case. In fact, 9 percent of *Sex and Psyche* respondents never thought of their regular partner during sex, and 19 percent thought of them not very often. Our fantasy partners can range from nameless men or women (who are won over by our prowess or just overcome by lust) to famous people, and, perhaps, neighbors, work colleagues, or friends.

"I have these fantasies about Ben Affleck," says Tracey, thirty-one. "Not the real actor, but this character he played in a movie where he's a bank robber. There's this scene where he can't sleep and does pull-ups on a bar by his bed, dressed only in his loose-fitting pajama bottoms. In the film, the scene can't last more than a few seconds, but in my fantasy it lasts much, much longer! There's another scene where he has sex with this assistant bank manager whose bank he just robbed, but he's gentle and considerate, even though he's got all these dragon tattoos across his shoulders and biceps. Sometimes, I look over my partner Rob's shoulders when we're having sex and pretend to trace those tattoos on his back with my fingers, although I'd hate it if Rob really did get some. I always climax really hard when I have this particular fantasy."

All of us, if we're honest, wonder how life would have turned out if we'd made different choices, stayed with an ex, taken a different career path, or married somebody else. Our sexual fantasies provide a reasonably safe environment to live out these alternate universes.

## Group Sex

If sex with one person is enjoyable, for many people in Kahr's survey, adding extra players into the fantasy makes it even better. In fact, 30 percent of his respondents fantasized about a threesome, 20 percent about attending an orgy, and 11 percent about swinging or partner swapping.

"They have these clubs in Paris called échangiste where couples explore their fantasies. I've never been, of course, just read a lot about them," Toby, thirty-five, told me. "It's not a tacky place, and my girlfriend is dressed up as if we were going to a five-star hotel. All the men in the club really want her, because she's the most beautiful and classiest woman in the place. So they keep on coming up to us at the bar, kissing her hand, and asking my permission to ravish her. We turn them away and enjoy our champagne cocktails and canapés. When the sexual tension from all these men with their tongues hanging out gets too much, I lead my girlfriend to a large bed and invite these men one by one to perform oral sex on her. When she's really hot, I allow a man to enter her, and after that it's open season and she takes them all on. Finally, when it's my turn, I am rough with her until we both have this enormous climax. When my girlfriend finally straightens up her clothes and makeup, and we leave, all the men in the club are jealous because she's going home with me."

Kahr, who is a Freudian psychotherapist, believes our personality is shaped by childhood experiences. According to him, people who enjoy group sex fantasies are likelier than the general population to have been brought up in a large family with extended family, including grandparents and aunts and uncles, helping to raise them. He also suggests that these fantasies assist in exploring repressed homosexual and lesbian desires.

## Homosexuality

In Kahr's research, 91 percent considered themselves heterosexual, 3 percent homosexual or lesbian, 4 percent bisexual, and 1 percent undecided. However, when he changed the categories for a pilot study (conducted by YouGov) of 3,617, the nation's sexuality became a little more fluid. Only 85 percent of the population considered themselves heterosexual, because 7 percent identified themselves as heterosexual but "bi-curious," and 1 percent as homosexual but "bi-curious."

It seems for many people their sexuality is a gray area, and when it comes to fantasies, we are even harder to categorize. For example, Patrick, twenty-four, imagines his best friend is sharing his girlfriend with him:

"In the fantasy, it's not his real girlfriend, but she's got large breasts and I'm masturbating between them while he's having sex with her. After a while we change over, and it's really nice being naked together, showing off our penises, and although we don't touch each other or anything, when I go down on her I can still taste him in her wetness."

At first sight, men who fantasize about two women making love would seem to be gold-standard heterosexuality. "I'm watching two gorgeous women make love, they don't know I am there, and as they get more turned on, I get more turned on until I can't help but moan. They spot me in the doorway and insist that I join in," says Timothy, thirty-six.

Ethel Spector Person, Professor of Clinical Psychiatry at Columbia University, believes that men imagine themselves as one of the women so there is no masculine competition—no brother, no father, and no boss. Kahr, however, believes that lesbian fantasies suggest that the man did not receive enough mothering when he was a child.

## Voyeurism

Unless our parents split up when we were very young, we grow up witnessing our parents' love affair (or lack of it). The health of their relationship is so important to our well-being that we are tuned in to every up and down, and notice every kiss and every cuddle. No wonder we grow up to have fantasies about peeping through keyholes and watching other people make love: 23 percent of the population have fantasized about watching two or more women having sex, 21 percent about watching a man and a woman having sex, 13 percent about spying on someone undressing, and 7 percent about watching two or more men having sex.

Ray, thirty-six, has a favorite voyeuristic fantasy:

"I'm living in one of those New York skyscrapers, and a beautiful woman with long flowing auburn hair moves into the apartment across the street. On the first night she forgets to draw her curtains, so I can see her undressing. Just as she's about to take off her bra and panties, she notices me watching. I don't turn away but pretend I'm enjoying the view of downtown. She doesn't get angry or close the curtains, just turns her back, slips off her bra, and disappears under the cover.

"The next night, I'm watching, and the same happens, except this time she's not wearing the bra and panties but a red corset and matching suspenders. The third night she strips completely and pushes her full breasts against the window, leaving steamy smudges. On the fourth, she shows off her butt and masturbates, licking her fingers and smearing them across the window. On the fifth night, the apartment is dark and empty. She's moved out, but I have climaxed by that point."

Many voyeuristic fantasies overlap with the next category.

## Exhibitionism

Exhibitionism is a healthy part of growing up. Boys show off their newly acquired biceps and most girls flaunt their breasts in tight tops or sweaters. So it is not surprising, perhaps, just how much further we are prepared to go in our fantasies. The *Sex and Psyche* survey showed that 8 percent of women have a fantasy of displaying their breasts and 4 percent of uncovering their genitals in public. Nineteen percent of the public have fantasized about being watched during sex. Eleven percent want an even larger audience and to star in a pornographic movie. The younger half of the survey was twice as likely to have exhibitionist fantasies.

There is something about modes of transportation that accompanies this type of fantasy. In my research, I've had reports of making love on top of cars (in the driveway of the man's girlfriend's parents), on the train, and, of course, in an airplane.

"In my fantasy, it is late at night. Most passengers are asleep and I'm standing at the galley chatting to one of the flight attendants," says Ross, thirty-four. "One thing leads to another, and we start kissing passionately. She whispers for me to come to the bathroom in five minutes, knock twice, and she'll let me in. When I follow her instructions, she's totally naked except for black stockings. Pretty soon, the whole plane is rocking. Suddenly, there's a knock on the door. Another passenger wants to use the toilet. 'Don't let that bother you. Come on! Come On!' she screams.

Afterward, she straightens her uniform and pushes past the man waiting to get into the toilet. He smiles because it must have been obvious what had been happening. As I walk back to my seat, all the passengers applaud and that's when I climax."

## Fetishism

Fetishism is defined as an erotic thrill provided by the presence of a physical item. The classic examples include rubber, leather, and high heels. Dressing up in the clothes of the opposite sex is popular in fantasies too, with 6 percent enjoying this fetish. The Internet has probably played a part in widening the number and type of fetishes. "Furries" like to dress up as animals or cartoon characters and some have special access points in the costume to facilitate sex. There is also a small subset that is aroused by stuffed toys. Other fetishes include balloons (blowing them up, sitting on them, and popping them with sharp objects), infantilism (wearing a diaper and being treated as a baby or a toddler, sometimes of the opposite sex), and sploshing (being aroused by foods or slimy substances, which are generously applied to naked skin).

Anita, twenty-eight, went to a summer music festival and on the spur of the moment agreed to mud wrestle with one of her friends. "There was nothing sexual at all; we laughed loads. But it must have sparked something because I started getting these fantasies. The lights are low and a huge inflatable bath has been filled with olive oil or something slippery and tasteless. I take off all my clothes, and I launch myself into this pit of wriggling bodies. Soon I'm covered in gunk and slipping and sliding over all these other limbs and shapes. I close my eyes and sink into this warm embrace of ever-moving, ever-changing flesh. Occasionally, I might brush up against a hard penis or a forgiving breast, but it's not about intimate body parts, rather something more primeval as if we're a bucket of eels."

## Humiliation

There is a high unlikelihood that the next few categories are disclosed. However, just because few people willingly admit to them does not mean they are not widespread. Although there is no specific category for humiliation in the *Sex and the Psyche* research, several humiliating fantasies are measured. Thirteen percent of the population fantasizes about being forced to masturbate. Nine percent enjoy the idea of forcing someone else to masturbate. Thirteen percent fantasize about being forced to strip, and 11 percent imagine forcing someone else to strip. Six percent fantasize about urinating on someone and 6 percent being urinated on.

Maggie, thirty-eight, is one of the people whose fantasies include an appearance by the Queen of England.

"It's late at night, and I'm looking around Buckingham Gallery or perhaps the Queen's Picture Gallery and there's this good-looking guy—perhaps he's an art critic because he's got glasses on and is peering at all the paintings. We get talking and the conversation turns from the semi-naked Madonnas and nymphs to my figure. He's very complimentary and has soon persuaded me to compare and contrast. One thing leads to another and we're naked on the bench in the middle of the gallery having passionate sex. Just as he's about to enter me, the Queen walks in. She is either enjoying a private late-night viewing of her paintings or taking a short cut to her quarters. She lets out a sharp intake of breath and you can tell she's not pleased that we've despoiled her home. We stand up, exposing our naked bodies, clutching our clothes. She claps her gloved hands and guards appear from nowhere and drag us away as we protest and apologize."

## Violence

On top of the violence implicit in a dominant or submissive fantasy, there are other people who enjoy the idea of pain, both giving and receiving it. Eighteen percent of British men and 7 percent of British women fantasize about spanking someone; conversely, 11 percent of men and 13 percent of women fantasize about being spanked. Seven percent are interested in using a whip, paddle, cane, slipper, or strap. Mandeep, thirty-three, is Sikh and his family does not know he is gay.

"I have this fantasy where I'm stripped to the waist, I've uncoiled my turban, and my hair falls down over my shoulders, even though I'm supposed to have my head covered in public. This skinhead, who also has his shirt off, appears and starts whipping my back. Lash after lash, I have no choice. I have to take it. He's really getting off on my cries for mercy, but he doesn't care. He just hits me harder and faster. Sometimes, I'm on the ground and he's kicking me with his steel-toe boots. The pain is incredible, but, in my fantasy, so is the pleasure, and I can't tell where one ends and the next begins."

## The Forbidden

Transgression is an important part of all fantasies, and as what is socially acceptable changes, so does the nature of our private psychodramas.

Take, for example, the work of the French author Raymond Radiguet (1903–1923), whose semi-autobiographical novel, *Le Diable au corps (The Devil in the Flesh)* is about a married woman who takes a fifteen-year-old boy as her lover. It caused a scandal when it was published in 1923, not because of the underage sex, as we would imagine, but because the woman was married to a soldier who was risking his life on the front line.

When many states in the U.S. had antimiscegenation laws that barred blacks and whites from marrying or having sex, interracial pornography was popular. With interracial marriage commonplace and political correctness taking hold, the new transgressive edge is "racial play," where race insults are added into sex.

For example, in Mandeep's fantasies the "skinhead" would shout the very taunts that young white men used when he was growing up. Other racist sexual scenarios include slave auctions and Nazi interrogations of Jews. Since the arrival of AIDS, where semen can be potentially life threatening, gay pornography and sex blogs have focused on actors and diarists seeing how many "loads" they can take anally or orally. It seems nothing is so forbidden that it cannot be fuel for fantasies.

Indeed, every category of fantasy flirts with taboos—even Sophie's tender lovemaking on the beach involves sex in a public place, and Scott's fantasy about the first time with his wife has undertones of dominance and submission. Although fewer people have transgressive fantasies about humiliation, violence, and bondage, they are by no means uncommon. In fact, only 38 percent of the population, according to Kahr, has *never* had one of these fantasies.

## WHY WE FANTASIZE

While our sexual fantasies reveal a lot about us, our reactions to other people's fantasies probably tell us even more. We are either horrified or become aroused and possibly even jealous because our own fantasies are not as sexually liberated. So it is no surprise that the experts are divided on this as well. In the first camp, there are the therapists who believe fantasies allow dark thoughts to be expressed harmlessly. In the second camp, they believe a violent fantasy is a sign that someone is struggling to deal with aggression in the nonsexual part of their lives and therefore needs treatment. Perhaps the best way to settle the argument is to look at the various roles fantasies can play in our lives. Once again, there is a degree of overlap.

## Self-soothing

Everybody fantasizes for different reasons, but at the core is one simple concept: sexual fantasies make us feel better about ourselves. Sophie, in her fantasy about making love to her partner on the beach, has a "perfect body," and Toby gets an ego boost from possessing the woman that every-body else desires at the sex club. Fantasies also relieve the boredom of daily life, provide a respite from our troubles, calm us, and help us fall asleep.

Olivia, in her late thirties, has one particular favorite: "It's the Super Bowl and the favored team is having a disastrous game. At half time, the quarterback heads to his locker room and finds me there partially clothed. We make wild passionate love, and he goes back to the field and wins."

I was not surprised to discover that Olivia had a dominant mother and low self-esteem. However, in her fantasies, she is not only extremely desirable but can turn around a football game.

## Play

Children are encouraged to play and be creative. Unfortunately, when we grow up and have to earn a living, play is seen either as a waste of time or codified into sports and competition. The sense of doing something just for the fun of it is lost for the majority of adults. So it is no surprise, really, that many fantasies echo childhood play: throwing food about, getting messy together, or becoming animals. In this light, Anita's bucket of eels sounds almost pre-sexual, just rolling on the floor and play wrestling with friends or kicking off shoes and socks and climbing into the sand pit.

In the creative industries, acting, advertising, writing, etc., people are encouraged to play games as a way of generating ideas. In our sexual fantasies, play can be another *bridge* between the adult worlds of paying bills, saving for vacations, and getting a good night's sleep and the childish ability to be in the moment and have fun together.

## Transition

One of the main tasks of growing up is to slowly separate from our parents. As we know from watching babies and small children, being apart from your mother can arouse plenty of anxiety. Donald Winnicott, an English pediatrician and psychoanalyst (1898–1971), studied interactions between mothers and children, in particular picking up and handling a baby, and how a mother could be metaphorically "holding" a child when she was not with the child. For example, by singing or talking to the baby from the next room, or providing what Winnicott called a "transitional object" (like a teddy bear) to offer symbolic mothering, a child does not feel entirely alone. It's the proverbial security blanket.

Our need to be "held" and kept safe explains the popularity of bondage (tying someone up or being tied up) and some of the other fetishes. In his study, Kahr tells the story of a man with an intrusive mother who, when he was a child, would burst into his bedroom without knocking and allowed him no private space. So he would masturbate in the cupboard under the stairs, surrounded by plastic raincoats and rubber Wellington boots. As an adult, his fantasies always had beautiful women in boots and rubber, as they were the "transitional objects" from his teenage solo pleasure into the complex adult world of relationships. Many sexual tastes are set even younger, almost pre-sexual, which explains the popularity of shoe and foot fetishes, as these objects are directly in the line of sight of small children.

## Wish Fulfillment

Many of our fantasies are simply better in our head, as Sophie found out when she went on vacation to Maui.

"The moon was glistening on the waves and our bodies, which was very romantic until we discovered it was also glistening off the backs of two or three hundred sea crabs. What's more, they seemed very curious about what we were doing and started crawling toward us."

Other fantasies, like Ross having sex on the airplane, would probably lose the flight attendant her job, lead to a lot of embarrassing questions, and maybe a jail sentence.

With a great number of fantasies, the people and the events are symbolic or about something else altogether. For example, I doubt Patrick really wants to share his friend's girlfriend—even his pleasure imagining showing off his penis is unlikely to be representative of unconscious homosexual desires. Such fantasies are normally about the need for recognition from a distant father.

Fantasies about someone much younger or from our past might not be an instruction from our subconscious to go out and find them but nostalgia for when we ourselves were young and firm.

Therefore, if you are thinking of turning a fantasy into reality—for example, starting an affair with a friend or work colleague—think twice. Although we place a lot of emphasis on going with our instincts or trusting our feelings, these are not necessarily a reliable guide to what's best for us. Studies by the psychologist Arthur Aron of New York's Stony Brook University suggest that stress hormones distort romantic perceptions. For example, the adrenaline rush that comes with the fear or the thrill of going against social conventions could be confused with the sensation of falling in love. In a nutshell, your fantasies are clues on how to act, not instructions.

## Avoidance of a Painful Reality

Imagining we're James Bond or Wonder Woman performing heroic or extraordinary feats in the bedroom is perfectly harmless. However, it can also stop us from facing up to painful realities like receding hairlines or sagging breasts. And the anxieties are not just about our looks.

Every man worries about satisfying his partner, whether consciously or unconsciously, and every woman has anxieties about being good enough. Instead of facing these fears and doing something practical about them, many people self-medicate through their sexual fantasies.

For example, Timothy, through his lesbian scenario, proves he is "all man" and has no problem maintaining an erection by satisfying not one woman, but two. What's more, his lesbian lovers are so turned on that they abandon each other and turn all their attention to Timothy. A common male anxiety is that it takes two penises to satisfy one woman. In the sex club fantasy, Toby compensates by going to the opposite extreme and offering his girlfriend to everybody in the club. None of those men can satisfy her; she has to wait for intercourse with Toby to orgasm.

In the same way, fantasizing about people other than your partner, especially if this is the only way you become aroused or achieve orgasm, might keep your sex life nominally alive, but avoids your having to look at the painful reality of the state of your relationship and making necessary changes.

## Early Warning System

There is a flip side to using fantasies to avoid painful reality: they can just as easily be an early warning system. Often, we are so busy earning a living, bringing up children, and running a home, that we don't realize that our life is somehow off-kilter. Over time, the stress mounts, but we tell ourselves that sleeping in on the weekend, a vacation, or completing a project at work will make it better. Although on the surface, everything is okay, underneath our body is crying out to stop, or our soul is facing an existential crisis because the gap between the life we need to lead and the one we're actually living has become too great. For other people, an event today will reawaken an unresolved crisis from the past, but instead of attending to it, they plough on anyway. Whatever the cause of the distress, our unconscious mind can start sending signals that surface through our sexual fantasies.

Russell, thirty-five, had always clicked with Ruth, a woman that he knew through work. He had occasionally fantasized about her, but the urge got stronger and stronger. "When my wife was giving birth to our third child, I kept seeing myself in the corner doing all sorts of wonderful things with Ruth. It was most unsettling."

Instead of wondering why the fantasies had become so powerful, Russell took them as straightforward signs and six weeks later started an affair with Ruth. In counseling, Russell finally admitted that he did not want to be a father again and that he longed to be free of his responsibilities. He had tried to tell his wife, but the taboo about not wanting or not loving your children was too strong. However, Russell's problems went deeper. When I looked at his birth order, I was not surprised to discover that he was the third child or that his parents split up when he was five years old. Russell immediately reached for the tissues and for the first time in our counseling sessions started to cry.

"What caused that?" I asked when his tears subsided.

"I guess I always wondered if I caused my parents' split. You know, the extra stress of three kids. The straw that broke the camel's back."

Russell had been carrying this burden for thirty years, and although his sexual fantasies had raised the alarm, he had chosen to ignore it. Fortunately, he confessed his infidelity to his wife and worked hard to resolve both his marriage and his personal issues. As often happens, voicing his fears was half the battle, and Russell went on to repair his relationship with both his wife and his newborn son.

## Mastery of Trauma

I never cease to be amazed at the creativity of the human mind and how many people use sexual fantasies, either consciously or unconsciously, to master an old trauma by turning a painful memory into a pleasurable one. Maggie's fantasy about being discovered by the Queen made complete sense when she told me about an event from her childhood.

"My mother was a feminist and believed that I should know about my body and how it functioned. So when I was about twelve, she gave me this book about sexuality. It was really interesting and inspiring, and I made myself this small dildo. I hid it in my dresser, but she found it and called me to my bedroom to inquire. I was so embarrassed. She knew I was lying about what it really was, and I knew she knew, but nothing more was ever said."

Through her fantasies, Maggie had turned a humiliating experience into a pleasurable one.

Mandeep's fantasies of being thrashed by a skinhead and sometimes baiting him to hand out more punishment takes his teenage fears of being attacked and subverts them. Instead of being a helpless victim, he is inviting the pain, and in a roundabout way, he is finally in control. Other people lessen past shame and humiliation through their sexual fantasies by becoming the person doling out the punishment.

A milder example of using fantasy to replay and heal old wounds comes from Hannah, forty-eight, whose first sexual experience was hurried, rough, and disappointing. "In my fantasies, I lose my virginity to the seventies pop star David Cassidy. He is kind and gentle. When I cry, he pats my eyes dry with a lace handkerchief. He also helps me tidy up afterward, rather than going off to watch football with his friends, like what happened in reality."

## Discharge of Aggression

Many fantasies are riddled with aggression about being "ridden hard like a horse and put away wet." Even romantic novels are full of violent images like "ripping her clothes off" and being "thrown onto the bed." As previously discussed, sex is about control and submission; a penis, tongue, or finger enters the vagina, mouth, or anus—so violation is always going to be part of the equation. However, on a deeper level, humans are aggressive creatures, and these socially unacceptable feelings have to be discharged somehow.

Sigmund Freud believed that our sexual fantasies serve as the fulfillment of primitive, unbearable wishes and protect our minds from all sorts of uncomfortable thoughts. However, Carl Jung talked about our shadow side: "The thing a person has no wish to be." Into this disowned part of ourselves, we deposit all the uncontrollable instincts, the destructive impulses, and the characteristics we consider unwanted or inferior.

Although everybody has a shadow side, most people deny or repress it.

One of the ways our anger toward our partner can leak out, in a relatively manageable form, is through our fantasies. For example, Derek making his wife satisfy every man in the sex club is very close to punishing her. It also begs a question about how well he deals with unresolved anger in his day-to-day life.

Michel Foucault (1926–1984), a French philosopher interested in sexuality and erotic transgression, went further and linked pain and pleasure. The idea is taken up by Geoff Mains in his book *Urban Aboriginals* (Gay Sunshine Press, 1984). In this sociological and anthropological study of the leather subculture in North America, Mains described how a mood of trust between partners (rather than brutal attack) and a gradual buildup of carefully and precisely placed pain can be transformed into sexual ecstasy.

In the mid-1970s, scientists had discovered natural chemicals in our bodies called endorphins and enkephalins. These are used by nerves to communicate with each other, activate the body's internal pain control system, and create a morphine-type substance in the brain responsible for a feeling of euphoria or trance. Mains explained that sadomasochism (or S&M) provided not only a safe way to discharge aggression, but that the associated endorphin rush triggered by beating, spanking, etc., increased practitioners' desire for more pain. Interestingly, he linked these relatively new sexual practices in America in the 1980s with ancient religious rites that promoted ecstasy like the Dervish (Sufi whirling dancers), Hopi Sun Dance (Native Americans who pierced participants' chests with pegs), and fire-walking (which can be traced back to the twelfth century BC and cultures as far apart as Greece and China).

## BALANCING ONESELF

Well-balanced people have less hidden in their shadow side. They have access to the whole range of human emotions and characteristics—from tenderness to aggression, controlling to vulnerable, nurturing to being nurtured, generous to selfish, and fixed to flexible. Unfortunately, society and culture give us all sorts of messages: big boys don't cry, nice girls don't enjoy sex, don't be too needy, don't show weakness. The list is endless, but the result is the same—the narrowing of the range of acceptable feelings. Furthermore, it is easy to get pigeonholed in a particular role and, for example, dedicate your life to looking after others (and forget that you have needs too).

One of the ways we cope with the contradictions of human nature—beyond shoving the parts we find unacceptable in our shadow side and forgetting them—is expressing the other parts of ourselves through fantasy and sexuality. Naomi is a respectable wife and mother, but her imaginary lovers are often rogues—the sort of boys that lived on other end of town when she was growing up and whom her mother had placed strictly off-limits.

One of her favorite sexual fantasies involves making love on a luggage carousel at Los Angeles Airport with the bad-boy character from her favorite soap opera. "These are men who don't play by the rules, great for a fling but not the kind who marry and have children."

> *"One of the ways we cope with the contradictions of human nature—beyond shoving the parts we find unacceptable in our shadow side and forgetting them—is expressing the other parts of ourselves through fantasy and sexuality."*

In effect, Naomi is wondering what would have happened if she had not settled down right after college. Although basically happy with her choices, she can compensate for lost opportunities with a rich fantasy life.

Ross, who dreamed of joining the "mile-high club," is generally unassuming and does not like to push himself forward at work. "It's safer being one of the back-room guys rather than one of the 'stars' in sales and having your neck on the line all the time." However, in his fantasies, he can satisfy his need for praise and attention by receiving a round of applause for seducing a beautiful flight attendant.

## Experimentation

When we were teenagers, touch alone was enough for us to feel desire. The older we become, the more important it is for our feelings, and, in particular, our thoughts and fantasies, to be in alignment before we can feel sexual. So as we learn more about ourselves, we need to be certain our sex life matches who we have become or would like to be. Unfortunately, this can involve making changes, and just the thought of this is overwhelming and challenging to many.

Jeanette, thirty-eight, had always considered sex something more for men than women. "When I stop and think about it, I got some pretty screwed-up ideas from my mother. First, it was my job to please my partner. Second, it wasn't ladylike to let yourself go too much," she explained during her counseling session.

"The first half sounds like a performance. The second half sounds like you shouldn't throw yourself into the role but hold back," I remarked.

"My husband and I masturbated together, like you suggested, and I showed just how I enjoyed sex. It was really wild, but afterward I felt dirty and ashamed."

"How would you like to be?"

"I don't know. Vocal, uninhibited."

"Active, not just lying there?" I asked.

Jeanette nodded and looked sad. The gap between how she behaved in bed and how she'd like to behave seemed unbridgeable. So I suggested allowing herself to fantasize, as this is a safe arena to experiment with ideas that we hope for or fear.

The next week Jeanette looked happier. "In my fantasy, I was moaning, gasping, and shouting all these obscenities to spur my husband on. It was such a turn-on that I couldn't help myself and moved up to meet his thrusts. My husband noticed the difference, and I think he was pleased."

Over time, Jeanette was able to bring more and more from her fantasy into her real lovemaking, but it is unlikely she would have had the confidence without trying the ideas out first in her head.

## Self-Punishment

There is sometimes an element of punishment for crimes real or imagined in our fantasies. For example, Mandeep did not feel completely comfortable with his homosexuality, so his skinhead fantasy allowed him to express his sexuality and be punished for it at the same time. Sometimes the reasons for self-punishment are more obscure. For example, some people experience humiliating or degrading fantasies after being promoted at work. Why should this be? Freud suggested that nobody wants to be more successful than their parents, so they unwittingly self-sabotage their careers or, more healthily, compensate for their promotion by being put down in their fantasies.

## Defense Against Intimacy

We all long to get close to someone. It is a basic human need. However, letting someone into our life makes us vulnerable to possible rejection or losing independence. Many people are profoundly uncomfortable with intimacy—normally due to a difficult childhood or their parents' divorce —and either have a series of short-term relationships with unavailable people or spend long chunks of time alone. I have counseled men who have one-night stands and short flings, but find solo masturbation with their fantasies provide the most satisfying orgasms. Alternatively, some widows feel a relationship with another man would be unfaithful and retreat into their fantasies, which often are based around memories of their deceased partner.

I have also met divorced men and women who have been so profoundly affected by their breakup that they retired from relationships altogether and get their closeness from their children and friends. Once again, fantasy plays a consolation role in their sex lives. (If this is your situation and you'd like to change it, there is more help in my book *Heal and Move On: Seven Steps to Recovering from a Breakup*).

## HOW FANTASIES CAN IMPROVE RELATIONSHIPS

For many of people, the reasons why they choose one fantasy over another is simply unimportant. "It works, so what?" However, fantasies are more than a window into the psyche; they are an important tool for creating a passionate and plentiful sex life in the following ways:

## Repair

When couples are having a disappointing love life, it is hard to communicate problems in a way that is both sensitive enough to keep delicate egos intact and clear enough to be effectively communicated and understood.

Dionne and Jacob, in their late thirties, were both teachers, although Dionne had been appointed principal of her school. They prided themselves on being a modern couple and tried to split childcare down the middle. The result was that Jacob was a very engaged father and had a close relationship with his children. In the counseling room, Dionne was forceful. "I don't want a relationship like my parents, where my father was a bully and my mother did everything to appease him."

Meanwhile, Jacob seemed to be the opposite of who Dionne said her father was. He was sensitive, understanding, and often glanced at Dionne before saying something he feared might be controversial. "Our sex life is adequate and fine when you consider the impact of having two children, but I don't think either of us really enjoys it," Jacob said tentatively. "I try to ask Dionne what she would like from me in the bedroom, but she says she doesn't want 'sex by numbers.'"

I had a picture of a desperate-to-please Jacob and an angry and resentful Dionne. To check my hunch, I asked about Dionne's promotion and whether she was under increased pressure. She nodded. I already knew that she did the majority of the disciplining of their two children and had the final say on most of the family matters. My suspicion was that although Dionne kept an iron fist over the rest of her life, with very little happening without her stamp of approval, she actually wanted to surrender the control in the bedroom (and thereby instill a balance in herself). Unfortunately, she could not articulate this need, felt it was politically incorrect, or that somehow Jacob should know what she needed. Rather than opening up a complex and potentially painful conversation, I decided to ask about her fantasies.

I was not surprised that Dionne climaxed to images of crusader knights—nasty, brutal, and selfish—who tied virgins to altars and took what they wanted. In effect, her fantasies were the complete opposite of her "polite" sex life.

"How could you incorporate those ideas into your lovemaking?" I asked at the end of the session. When they returned the next week, I could tell from their body language that things had gone well.

"I told Dionne, 'Get up those stairs and I'll give you something to cry about,'" said Jacob. "I meant it half in jest but actually it was a complete turn-on. And who would have thought that thinking about my own needs was much sexier than ignoring them?"

## Subversion

Despite the feminist revolution and men becoming more aware of their feelings, many myths about sex are still alive and well. For example, men are in charge of sex and should have all the knowledge (and any lack is somehow "unmanly"), and women are responsible for pleasing a man (and taking charge is somehow not feminine). Playground messages about sex are still incredibly unhealthy. A teenage boy who has lots of partners is a "stud" (and revered by his friends) and a teenage girl is "easy" (ostracized by all, or subjected to bullying and verbal putdowns). No wonder sex—even in loving relationships—is incredibly complicated. Fortunately, fantasies provide a way to "play" with these messages and ultimately subvert and extinguish them.

Daniel, thirty, and Katie, thirty-two, had been together for three years when the shine came off their relationship and, fearing that they'd fallen out of love, came to counseling. Their sex life was routine and uninteresting. In a nutshell, Daniel was in control and Katie surrendered. What would happen if Daniel just laid back and let Katie take control?

"It seems rather selfish not to give her pleasure," said Daniel.

"So what?" I replied. "It's not forever, just a little experiment."

"It might be fun," added Katie with a gleam in her eyes as she went on to talk about some of the sex toys she still had from her single days.

"Why haven't you used them with Daniel?" I asked.

"I didn't want him to think I was that kind of girl or, I suppose, to feel threatened," she explained.

"So now do you think less of her?" I asked Daniel.

Daniel shook his head.

They returned the next week and explained how Katie used her vibrator to explore around Daniel's scrotum and the perineum. She also held the vibrator against the underside of his penis.

"The pleasure was so intense, I tried to stop her," said Daniel.

"But I knelt on one hand and held him down with the other," said Katie.

She had been in control and he had surrendered, and they had both subverted their respective sexual stereotypes. It was like watching them throw off a layer of protective armor and becoming truly intimate and therefore more loving again.

## Expansion

If you ate the same diet every day for years, you would get bored and long for something different and unexpected. Yet couples will have the same sort of sex as when they were first married, even if that was twenty or more years ago. Fortunately, we seem to be expanding our range, according to the National Survey of Sexual Health and Behavior at Indiana University (*Journal of Sexual Medicine,* October 2010). They identified more than forty combinations of sex acts but pared them down to five basic categories: penile-vaginal intercourse, solo masturbation, mutual masturbation, oral sex, and anal sex. Amazingly, 6 percent of men twenty-five to twenty-nine claimed to have indulged in all of them the last time they slept with someone. Sixteen percent of eighteen- to twenty-four-year-olds and 8 percent of women age fifty to fifty-nine reported using four of the five techniques the last time they had sex.

"The findings demonstrate the enormous variability that occurs in the sexual repertoire," says Debby Herbenick, one of the report's authors. "Vaginal intercourse was still the most common sexual behavior but we have an evolving and varying definition of what it means to have 'had sex.'" Indeed, when the National Health and Social Life Survey (NHSLS) was carried out by researchers at Chicago University in 1988, 12 percent of American women age twenty-five to twenty-nine had experienced anal sex in the last year, whereas that figure almost doubled to 21 percent in the NHSLS. (This figure also applies to thirty- to thirty-nine-year-olds.)

Fantasy is a particularly useful gateway to expanding your repertoire of sexual activities and preventing boredom in the bedroom. After Ray discussed his skyscraper voyeurism fantasy with his partner, she agreed to strip and then tease him by pleasuring herself while he watched. Meanwhile, Anita, who had a fantasy about being in a bucket of eels after mud wrestling, had a naked food fight with her partner and they licked each other clean.

> *"Fantasy is a particularly useful gateway*
> *to expanding your repertoire."*

## WHAT TO DO IF FANTASIES ARE TROUBLING YOU

For most people, fantasies are sources of harmless pleasure; however, for a significant portion of the population, fantasies are deeply disturbing.

One of the reasons may be that fantasies can involve other people, and this feels like, in the words of former President Jimmy Carter in his famous 1976 *Playboy* interview, "committing adultery in my heart many times." Personally, I think even the happiest marriages need private space. Otherwise, we are overwhelmed by the day-to-day intimacy of living together and raising a family.

If you find your fantasies suddenly becoming more frequent, out of control, out of your norm, or you begin to desire other people, it does not necessarily mean that your relationship is in crisis. It does suggest, however, that something is off-kilter. Possibilities include midlife crisis, bereavement, career doldrums, depression, drinking, a new baby, or unresolved issues with your partner.

With aggressive and transgressive fantasies, the picture is more complicated. Imagining watching other people make love is fine, but peeping through the neighbor's bedroom curtains is a gross invasion of their privacy. Getting turned on by the thought of putting someone over your knee and spanking him or her is harmless, but forcing someone to submit is assault.

The key question is what purpose your fantasies serve. On one hand, they could be a way of balancing yourself, mastering trauma, or safely discharging negative emotions. Therefore, they could actually reduce the risk of committing an illegal, immoral, or harmful act. But repeatedly masturbating or having sex while imagining aggressive or transgressive acts could reinforce the fantasies to such a point that someone starts seeking out specialist pornography, which, in turn, can normalize something "forbidden" and encourage crossing the line between fantasy and reality.

If you are concerned that you might be falling into the second category, ask yourself three questions about the activity that you are considering:

1. Is it safe? Are you likely to spread life-threatening conditions like HIV or hepatitis C? Could someone be damaged or hurt? Is the humiliation and pain symbolic or pleasurable?

2. Is it sane? (Are you breaking the law?)

3. Is it consensual? Does your partner freely agree to explore your fantasies or are you putting undue pressure on him or her? Alternatively, are you going behind your partner's back in which case there would be no consent? Think through all the issues about consent, as it is more complex than it appears on its surface. (For example, if you decide to have exhibitionist sex, there is a difference between going to a club where membership implies consent and having sex in a public place where anyone could stumble across you, and therefore it is impossible to gain consent from passersby.)

Ultimately, if your fantasies are troubling you, speak to your doctor and seek the advice of a specialist. Ignoring your concerns can result in harm to yourself and/or others.

## SHARING FANTASIES WITH YOUR PARTNER

Sex is such a personal matter that just talking about it seems terribly exposing. Therefore, most people's automatic response is to keep their fantasies to themselves, partly because they are private and partly because they are worried about stirring up a hornet's nest of questions: *Will my partner still love me if he or she knows about my "dark" side? Will he or she be insanely jealous? What if my partner isn't jealous? Can I cope with my partner's dark side?*

Yet playing it safe and holding back feelings is how most couples fall into the polite sex trap, where lovemaking is more about obligation than passion. So how do you decide what is best for your relationship?

Naomi, married for almost twenty years with two teenage children, believes that fantasies should remain private. "Just because you've entered into a legal contract with someone does not mean that they own your fantasies. I've never cheated on my husband, but I think it would be a failure of the imagination if I went to a party and did not imagine how someone would look like without their clothes or weren't ambushed by wild exciting thoughts."

Even if her fantasies did not include real people whom her husband had just met, she would still not share them. "It's my private space," she explains. "A room of my own."

Ultimately, it is easy to list reasons for not sharing fantasies, and the decision is highly personal, but if you hope to bridge the gap in your sexual and intimate relationship, it is far more interesting to do so by exploring fantasies together.

Even if you partner is naturally jealous or wedded to partner-focused sex, it is still possible to reframe your fantasies so he or she feels like a priority or doesn't feel threatened. For example, Elaine, the trance lovemaker whom we met in the last chapter, had fantasies about being ravished by anonymous hands and tongues. She knew that if she told Rick, who was partner-focused, he would think that he wasn't enough for her. So instead of sharing her fantasy, I suggested Elaine think about how she could incorporate the fantasy into their lovemaking.

"What if he blindfolded me, so I couldn't see?" she said. "I would be more at the mercy of my other senses like touch and sound. He could walk around the room, and I wouldn't know where he was, when he'd be about to touch me or where. That would be a real turn-on."

So instead of sharing her specific fantasy, Elaine shared an idea inspired by it and returned the next week with news about how it had gone.

"It was better than I imagined," she said. "We slowly and lovingly undressed each other downstairs in front of the fire. Rick then blind-folded me, and I was completely at his mercy. He had to guide me up the stairs and help me find the bed. The level of trust between us was incredible, and I was right, my other senses were really heightened. Afterward, we agreed that we must do it again."

In the end, it did not matter where the idea came from or how they came to enjoy sex blindfolded.

Other couples sanitize their fantasies or do not spell them out fully. For example, Dionne's fantasy about crusader knights and helpless virgins is actually a rape fantasy, although neither she nor Jacob used this word. These kinds of fantasies are quite common. Researchers Lisa Pelletier and Edward Herold from the University of Guelph in Ontario found that 51 percent of women have fantasies of being forced to submit sexually. This research was duplicated by Donald Strassberg and Lisa Lockerd from the University of Utah who studied 137 college women and found that the women with fantasies about being forced experienced less guilt about sex and were open to a wider variety of experiences than those who did not have such fantasies.

There are some circumstances when it is easier to share fantasies. These include the recovery period from an affair. When everything in a couple's love life is out in the open, there is nothing to lose, and things are up for negotiation. Similarly, after a couple has been on the brink of splitting up, I find both partners want to find new ways to relate. Other opportunities, surprisingly enough, include pregnancies. Many couples worry that sexual intercourse will damage the fetus (even though this is not the case, unless the woman has a history of cervical weakness or a low-lying placenta) but still want to be sexually intimate. If you do decide to rule out intercourse during pregnancy, this can be a good time to explore fantasies and expand your repertoire.

Finally, reading a book like this one can be the catalyst for developing "erotic intelligence" and discovering something new about your own, or your partner's, sexuality.

# FANTASY TÊTE-À-TÊTE

If you decide that opening up a dialogue with your partner about fantasies would benefit your sex life, here are some pointers to help keep the discussion private, positive, and productive:

- Have a clear sense of what your fantasies are about and what you are trying to achieve before talking to your partner. Otherwise, there is a danger that he or she might misunderstand your request or become turned off by something incidental.

- Practice "appreciative inquiry," which begins a conversation with compliments celebrating the positive aspects of a relationship, before tackling the issues you want to fix. Starting off with the "good news," by telling your partner what you enjoy about your current sex life, instead of the "bad news," keeps things focused, nonjudgmental, and less defensive.

- These conversations are best conducted away from the bedroom and never after an argument or unsuccessful lovemaking.

- Share the basic outline of your fantasy or the desired new ingredient for your sexual repertoire.

- Ask your partner how he or she feels about your fantasy, encouraging him or her to feel safe to share his or her own.

- Once you both shared your thoughts about fantasy, you can begin to discuss the details and how it might be possible to incorporate them (or aspects of them) into reality.

- Do not mistake your partner's reservations or request for "time" to think things over as an outright no. That is you projecting your fear of rejection. To learn more about navigating this issue, refer to the First Impressions Cards in the exercise section.

- Accept that your partner will have different fantasies and just because they are not identical is not a catastrophe. Give each other the benefit of the doubt when something is unclear or uncertain and keep talking.

- Be flexible. Your fantasy does not have to be realized to the letter. Maybe your partner's reservations will prompt you to rethink and promote ideas that could be even more satisfying.

## TWO WEEKS OF EXPANSION

The previous exercises and tasks up to this point have allowed you to strip down your lovemaking to the basics of touching and kissing, improve communication, and slowly build up to intercourse again. This part of the program goes to the root causes of marital sexual boredom and shows how to keep challenging yourself and your partner to be more open, more intimate, and bring more of yourself into the bedroom.

Hopefully, thus far, this chapter has already fired up your imagination about new elements to introduce into your lovemaking and/or you might be considering visiting an adult entertainment store or website together. Regardless of how brave or creative you might be feeling, the good news is you have both re-sexed your relationship by changing the way you think and talk about sex as well as how you see each other as sexual beings. So what do you do to ease yourself into your new-and-improved roles? Try Two Weeks of Expansion, aimed at taking baby steps that will continue to keep you and your partner sharing and, most important, talking.

*Partner A chooses:* In the first week, Partner A is in charge and will make suggestions for something that you have either never done before or not for a long time. This can range from an activity or incorporating a spicy extra ingredient—for example, food, dirty talk, dressing up, or using particular props, toys, or equipment. Partner B will do his or her best to go along with the idea. If reservations rise about Partner A's suggestion,

Partner B should talk through any fears, rather than dismiss the idea. If there is a stumbling block, how could it be overcome or how could the idea be modified? Compromise here is key.

*Partner B chooses:* In the second week, Partner B is in charge and makes suggestions. Partner A does his or her best to go along with the experiment or find a way to embrace the underlying idea.

*Follow up:* Discuss what you enjoyed about each other's choices and whether there is anything you'd like to incorporate into your regular lovemaking.

Please be kind to each other. It takes courage to open up, and you might find this exchange alone facilitates closeness and sensuality. If you have trouble deciding who goes first, flip a coin.

Finally, if you come up with some simple but effective ideas that might appeal to other readers of this book, please share your experiences on my website: www.andrewgmarshall.com.

## SOMETHING TO SLEEP ON

**In summary, remember:**

- Fantasy can be a useful resource for keeping desire alive. Ultimately, your imagination is your most powerful sexual organ.

- Fantasy helps us embrace the inherent paradox of sex: It can be pure and raunchy; tender and carnivorous; primitive and spiritual; about losing yourself and finding yourself; something that can fill you up and leave you drained and empty.

- Sometimes what frightens us the most is the very thing that needs doing.

- Stability and staying in your comfort zone leads to boredom, resentment, and insecurity.

- Challenge, growth, and novelty lead to passion, trust, and commitment.

# SEX ED

**EXERCISE 17    DEFINING SEX**

When Bill Clinton swore under oath that he did not have sexual relations with Monica Lewinsky, he was telling the truth, even though she had performed oral sex on him and he had pleasured her with his cigar. In the strict legal sense, he did not have sexual relations because that is defined as penile-vaginal intercourse, but most of us would certainly consider their activities as sex. What is the definition of "sex" for you and your partner?

On many occasions at the beginning of counseling, I have new couples report that they have not made love for three months or more, but later discover they have masturbated each other or had oral sex during this supposedly barren time. "Doesn't that count as sex?" I ask as they blush and nod. Time and again, couples underreport or dismiss part of their lovemaking because they have not specifically labeled it as sex.

These days, I present couples with the target diagram (Figure 1 on the following page) to help them think about every activity that might constitute sex. In order to be clear where their boundaries lie, I also ask people to add activities that land just over the border and which they don't consider sexual at all.

To give you some ideas, look at Figure 2 on the following page. This shows what constitutes sex for Luke, a forty-one-year-old heterosexual in a five-year relationship.

At the center, Luke wrote: "Intercourse, oral sex, and mutual masturbation." In the second circle, he put "anal sex," which included occasionally penetrating his girlfriend Halle's anus with his penis and her putting her finger in his anus to massage his prostate gland while she masturbated him. I asked him why he'd put it here, and he explained that it was not really part of their usual lovemaking, but more a spicy extra. In the outer circle, he put voyeurism (which

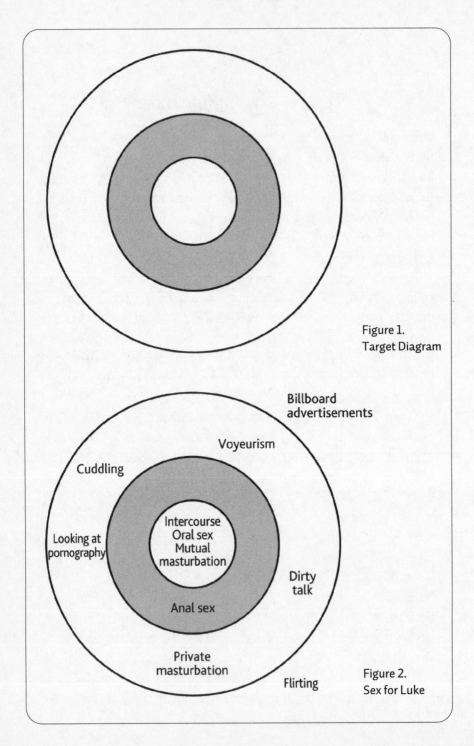

Figure 1.
Target Diagram

Billboard
advertisements

Voyeurism

Cuddling

Looking at
pornography

Intercourse
Oral sex
Mutual
masturbation

Anal sex

Dirty
talk

Private
masturbation

Flirting

Figure 2.
Sex for Luke

included activities that were not specifically erotic, but still intimate, like watching Halle towel herself after a long bath or cut her toenails), dirty talk (on the phone when he was away on business), private masturbation, looking at pornography (mainly on his own but sometimes with his girlfriend), and cuddling (intimate touching but not leading to arousal). Outside the target, he put activities that might provide a flicker of desire but did not, for him, constitute sex: flirting (telling a colleague she looked nice at a party) and billboard advertisements (semi-naked women on posters). Remember, this was just Luke's definition of sex. There is no right or wrong answer.

How do you use this information? First, it is a really good way of starting an intimate conversation with your partner. For example, Halle did not realize how much Luke enjoyed watching her get a pedicure or other beauty treatments, nor how important he viewed dirty talk when they were apart. Second, acquiring information helps couples expand their repertoire of activities. Luke and Halle, for example, decided to experiment with the idea of foot fetishism. Third, it helps get away from the idea that sex equals intercourse and everything else is second fiddle.

## EXERCISE 18    FIRST IMPRESSIONS CARDS

Discussing something new, personal, and revealing is always going to create anxiety. Many times in my counseling room, clients will begin to make a suggestion for improving sex but pull back, worried about the reception from their partners. Often, what they perceive as hostility is just their partners thinking about how to respond. To get around this problem I developed "First Impressions Cards." They allow the partner listening to give an instant reaction without committing themselves to their initial response, thereby reducing the stress of the proposing partner and improving overall communication. Once over this hurdle, these couples had no problems discussing their reservations and finding a way to make something enjoyable for both of them.

Create the cards below and put them on a table between the two of you. After the person making the suggestion has outlined the basic idea, the other picks up the most appropriate card and explains her reasoning.

**YES**

**YES**

With some reservations

**YES**

With lots of reservations that we have to discuss and overcome

**MAYBE**

**NO**

With reservations that could possibly be overcome

**NO**

With lots of regret

At any point in the subsequent discussion and clarifications, either partner can pick up a card to express his or her state of mind.

# Chapter Eight

# The Heart of the Matter

Every couple can benefit from talking more openly and honestly about sex, removing bad habits, and becoming more sensual. However, for some people, these are not enough to solve all of their issues and they need more specialized help. So in the final part of this book, I'm going to examine the most common situations that undermine sexual happiness. Even if none of these apply directly to your relationship, there are some useful insights into how your body works and the interaction between your brain and your genitals.

In the next chapter, I will cover a recent affair, pornography use, and past sexual abuse, but first I'm going to focus on issues of sexual functioning. These are often labeled as "medical" but are far more likely to originate in one's head rather than in the penis or the vagina. (However, it is important to stress that you should still consult your doctor and check that everything is functioning correctly and whether any of your current medications have side effects that might be contributing to your problems.)

## MY PARTNER HAS LOW LIBIDO

When a woman gives birth to a child, she produces more oxytocin in her brain, which is designed to encourage bonding, nurturing, and nursing her child. This increased level of oxytocin can keep a mother so focused on her child that she reports "mommy brain," the inability to concentrate on other things like work, relationships, hobbies, and chores. Among the most reported neglected areas during this time is sex, because many women experience a low or nonexistent libido, as their priority is their child. For many women, the increased levels of oxytocin will last for two years before waning, at which point the hormone vasopressin is increased and women can begin to feel more sexual again. In this manner, biology has encouraged women to desire sex to produce a child about every two years.

Dr. Glyn Hudson-Allez, a psychosexual therapist and author of the training guide for counselors *Sex and Sexuality,* believes that once women have had as many children as they want, their overall sexual desire drops, regardless of hormone levels. "Instead of being spontaneously horny, as they might have been before they had children, they become sexually responsive. In effect, their partner has to push the right buttons for them to be sexual. They are less likely to be rushing around feeling up for it."

Men also produce oxytocin, and Dr. Hudson-Allez explains the main difference between men and women and how oxytocin reacts in them by saying: "When men have sex with a long-term partner, it is part of showing their love. So when women say, 'I don't want it,' men feel personally rejected because it is their love that has been turned down."

This is possibly because, as we have discovered, ejaculation is the only time when men produce oxytocin. "For women," Dr. Hudson-Allez adds, "sex becomes an optional extra as they are showing their love with all the other things they're doing in the relationship."

Whatever oxytocin's impact on the human body, babies have a dramatic effect on sex lives, and not just because they are exhausting and time consuming. Bathing a baby, changing diapers, carrying him or her around, playing together, and rocking him or her to sleep are all incredibly intimate acts and involve lots of skin-to-skin contact. When you have infants, there are numerous ways to meet the human need for closeness. No wonder some mothers say about sex that they could "take it or leave it." On one level they are getting their emotional and bonding needs met elsewhere.

Tania, twenty-eight, had two small children and a new baby, and her life revolved around caring for them. "We've got three beautiful children and Benjamin is a great dad. Okay, we had a rocky patch because he doesn't see the practical things that need to be done—he'd rather be playing with his daughters than doing laundry—but that's been dealt with and things run smoothly enough. I've got a lot to be grateful about, but . . ."

"Your sex life is not very rewarding," I suggested.

"Nobody with three small children expects it to be."

"So why are you so angry?" I asked.

A torrent of complaints about housework and not being appreciated tumbled out, along with some tears.

"You don't feel special or cared for yourself," I empathized. "What would it feel like to be cherished and wanted?"

"Wonderful."

"That is what good lovemaking is all about," I explained.

In effect, Tania might have been getting her needs for physical closeness met by looking after her children, but it is only part of the story. We need adult intimacy too, where, of course, we give but also *receive*. In effect, a rewarding sex life replenishes some of the emotional energy that we expend while caring for children and helps keep us sane. Tania needed to shift how she perceived sex.

"More often than not, sex was something I did for Benjamin rather than for myself. If I was really stressed, it was just one more thing on my mental to-do list."

However, once they started the Month of Sensuality when lovemaking focused on being held, stroked, and soothed, Tania relaxed and let go of her stress.

"Previously, he just climbed on top and off he went, but now sex is for me too. It helps me feel better if I've had a tough day or feel a bit crappy because Benjamin is giving me a break from 'baby world,' and I'm reminded that I am still a passionate woman rather than solely a mom."

Another time when women can be less interested in sex is after a hysterectomy. Experts are divided on the reasons why. Some consider it to be part of a psychological adjustment, partly mourning the loss of fertility and partly reassessing what it means to be a woman. Others, like Rik van Lunsen, head of the Department of Sexology and Psychosomatic Gynecology at the University of Amsterdam, believe that sexual arousability or, how likely a woman is to respond to sexual stimuli, is dependent on androgen (a naturally produced steroid) and suggest taking supplements after a hysterectomy. Similarly, van Lunsen thinks hormone-replacement therapies for menopausal and postmenopausal women can reduce the levels of androgen in the body.

There is a third reason why couples arrive in counseling with different levels of desire. Alan Riley, professor of sexual health at the University of Central Lancashire in the United Kingdom, has analyzed a large number of people and their range of arousal. He plotted a graph from those with the lowest amount of desire to the highest and found that the majority of the population lies in the middle. However, Professor Riley noted that women score on the lower end of sexual desire and men score on the higher end. A relationship between an average man and woman will show a discrepancy in how often they want to have sex. If he is pressuring her and she is going through the motions to keep him quiet, it is possible that she will never reach the point of spontaneously desiring her partner.

Lauren, thirty-four, had, in her words, "gone off it," although she would consent to having sex to keep her partner happy. Brian knew that pressuring Lauren was counterproductive but kept making advances anyway because "I never know when I'm going to get lucky." Although Brian was getting sex about every ten days, he was dissatisfied. "I don't think my wife is really attracted to me. It's always me who has to ask. How do you think that makes me feel about myself?"

My suspicion was that Lauren found sex a duty rather than a pleasure because she had never had the breathing space for her desire to reach a sufficient level to either initiate sex or to benefit from the release of an orgasm.

So I asked Brian, "What would happen if you didn't ask for sex?"

"She'd never want it."

"Does she now?" I asked.

"Not really. She does it for me."

With reluctance, Brian agreed to an experiment. He would not ask for sex, drop hints, or pass remarks. Instead, he would wait until Lauren approached him.

"I'll have blue balls by that time," he joked.

"That's just the sort of crude remark that turns me right off," said Lauren.

When they came back next week, Lauren had not initiated sex. I had warned Brian that Lauren might take a "vacation" from lovemaking. However, Brian was not as frustrated as I had expected.

"She might not have wanted sex," he reported, "but she came and cuddled on the sofa. It was really nice, and I felt so close to her."

It took two weeks before Lauren felt enough desire to ask Brian for sex. "I can't tell you how wonderful it was when she led me upstairs by the hand," said Brian.

"Just before we finished, I screamed loud enough for half the street to hear," joked Lauren.

Lynne, thirty-two, and Michael, thirty-four, who had two children ages eleven and seven, arrived in counseling because Lynne had fallen out of love with Michael. Although they seldom argued (see my book *I Love You but I'm Not in Love with You* for more about the link between anger suppression and general lack of passion), it was clear that the major problem was an absence of desire. "It's nothing personal," Lynne told Michael. "Brad Pitt could walk in here and I wouldn't be interested."

Unfortunately, Michael enjoyed sex a lot. "I really love my wife. I think she's beautiful, and I want to make love to her. What's wrong with that?"

The problem had come to a head when Lynne finally started to refuse sex and asked for a separation. Halfway through their general counseling, I put Michael and Lynne on the program in this book, banned sex (which Michael found amusing), and introduced the nonsexual touching exercises. After two weeks on the program, they returned with a guilty secret.

"I found myself so turned on by touching Michael that I jumped him," said Lynne.

"I told her that we shouldn't, but I couldn't stop her. It was wonderful and we made love," Michael confessed.

In effect, Lynne had been given enough time without being pressured into sex to become spontaneously aroused and experience her own desire again (rather than succumb to his).

"I just couldn't understand what was wrong with me," Lynn said. "I'd wondered if I was a lesbian because I'd stopped wanting my husband, or any men, but I knew that wasn't the case. Then, I thought it was that I'd fallen out of love but actually I'd been turned off by years of feeling pressured and resentful."

They left counseling feeling not only "in love" again but like a honeymoon couple.

## CALLING A TRUCE IN THE WAR OF
## HIGH DESIRE VS. LOW DESIRE

When couples have a poor or nonexistent sex life, it is easy for one partner to be labeled as the "problem." This is especially the case when one partner (typically the man, but not always) would like more sex and points the finger at the other for ruining his (or her) love life. Blaming someone never helps the issue, and the fact of the matter is the entire picture is far more complicated. I prefer to remove the label and reframe the problem as a shared one.

The University of Quebec took forty couples with low sexual desire and compared them with a control group to look into the possible causes. In particular, they measured the link between low libido and depression, anxiety, and general compatibility (across nine indicators, including household tasks, money, social activities, and rearing children). The result was a strong link between loss of desire and dissatisfaction with the relationship in general, a moderate link between loss of desire and anxiety, and a weak link between low libido and depression. In other words, problems specific to the relationship outside the bedroom were being expressed inside the bedroom.

*"Problems specific to the relationship outside the bedroom*
*were being expressed inside the bedroom."*

Therefore, my first step in treating couples is to broaden the high desire/low desire debate away from sex. In every area of married life, one partner has a greater motivation for doing things than the other. For example, arranging social activities, getting the children to bed, disciplining the children, entertaining visitors, cleaning and maintaining the house, and budgeting are not usually equally distributed between partners. In many cases, the person who is reporting low levels of desire in the bedroom has high levels of desire to do some or all of the aforementioned things.

If you are the person with high libido in the relationship, can you consider an area of contention between you and your spouse, for instance, doing laundry, paying the bills, working two jobs, bath and reading time, mowing the lawn, or making the bed? Why do you think your partner feels frustrated and angry? Does it motivate you or does it make you less likely to cooperate? How does it feel to be the low desire partner in this area? Do you feel like you do nothing right or that anything that you do will not be valued? Are you doing to your spouse outside the bedroom the very thing you're accusing him or her of doing to your sex life?

I also help my clients reframe the war between low and high desire by explaining that men and women are asking each other for the same things, closeness and intimacy, but in completely different ways. Generally, a woman will ask for more communication, emotion, and romance. A man will ask for more sex. The discrepancy between men and women is due to how each gender is socialized.

Although things are changing, boys are still being taught to repress their feelings, solve their own problems, and be strong. The only socially acceptable way for a man to "be a man" and get close to his partner is through sex. Girls, by contrast, are still taught to make connections and share feelings and thoughts to create bonds and are warned about men who "want only one thing." Therefore, the best way to call a truce is to understand the similarities in each other's desire instead of concentrating on the differences.

Both partners need to learn to communicate a little bit of each other's way. In other words, the high sexual desire partner must spend more time talking and listening, while the low sexual desire partner comes to value sex as a way of communicating. (If you are the lower desire partner and this idea makes you anxious, refer to the exercise titled "Simmering" at the end of this chapter.)

# MALE-SPECIFIC
# SEXUAL DIFFICULTIES

Although in most long-term relationships, it is each partner who has made an equal, albeit different, contribution to the couple's general sexual unhappiness, there are some instances when one partner's specific problem undermines the couple's sexual happiness.

What I'm going to say next is often hard to accept, so please bear with me. Just like in the debate about low and high desire, I believe that even when the sexual difficulty is specific to the male or female, it should be perceived as a shared problem. Just because the issue happens to be exhibited in one person does not dismiss the other from responsibility. You can probably imagine the look of surprise on the faces of couples when I offer this viewpoint in sessions. It's a combination of relief that one of them might not be to blame and puzzlement, since, after all, it's his or her body that won't cooperate. At this point, I ask my couples to trust in the idea because as we begin to unravel their sexual problems, I can explain why I believe so strongly that sexual problems are synonymous with relationship problems, i.e., shared between the couple. Now I ask you to do the same and read both sections on male- and female-specific sexual issues before labeling yourself or your partner as "the problem."

At the heart of sexual dysfunction is a set of myths and expectations that men and women believe. So beginning with male-specific sexual issues first, I need to draw from the socialization of men. Men have been brought up to be strong, self-reliant, and successful on the sports field, the boardroom, and the bedroom. If something goes wrong, a man has to pick himself up, figure it out, and move on without complaint. Any man who fails to live up to these ideals is not only weak (possibly the worst insult that you can throw at him), but worse, is somehow not a man at all. Sure, it's acceptable not to be good at sports, as long as one compensates by excelling in the business world, but the one arena in which it is simply unforgivable to fail is the bedroom. Men have to know all the right moves, keep an erection, and give their partner an orgasm. That's a lot of responsibility to have on one's shoulders (or more accurately, one's penis), so the primary goal of sex in the mind of many men is to perform well rather than feel pleasure and closeness. Into the mix throw a set of myths about men and sex that are not only hard to live up to, but don't necessarily lead to great lovemaking (and in many cases actually undermine it), including:

- Men are supposed to know everything about sex.

- Men are always ready and interested.

- A real man makes the earth move for his partner.

- Sex is centered on the penis.

- A penis should be a foot long and made of steel.

Anxiety leaps off this posting on my website from a thirty-year-old virgin. "I'm not bad looking; in fact, I have nothing to worry about there, but I worry because I've not only never had sex but never had a girlfriend."

Like all men, he has to reassure me about his masculinity. "I have a successful career and no lack of personal achievement (and am well-educated with a post-grad degree). I can talk to women for hours, as long as I'm not trying to hook up, but I have no confidence in approaching women I like. I become a wreck. My parents want me to find a wife, but what am I supposed to do? If I do meet someone, what am I going to tell her about my history, or lack of it?"

Here is another letter from a thirty-seven-year-old man: "I am very worried that I will be a virgin for the rest of my life, and that is driving me crazy! Could you offer me even the remotest possibility of any hope? Also, because I am totally inexperienced in the art of love, I don't have very much knowledge of how to be a good lover, for example, I don't know how to kiss passionately."

The myth of men knowing everything about sex makes it simply inconceivable for these correspondents to tell a potential girlfriend about their situation and let her initiate them into the joys of lovemaking. Worse, this ignorance about sex can put men at risk. I had a twenty-nine-year-old client (once again with a post-graduate degree) who discovered a woman with whom he'd recently had a one-night stand was two months pregnant. "The news gave me a nasty shock, but I don't think I'm in the blame because although I didn't use a condom, I did withdraw in time," he told me.

I had to inform him that semen is present in pre-ejaculatory fluid.

However, the most pernicious myth of all is that sex is centered on the penis. It not only reinforces the idea that real sex equals intercourse (and somehow anything else is second best), it drives many of the most common sexual problems for men *and* women, beginning with the next one—erectile dysfunction.

## Erectile Dysfunction

There is immense pressure on men to maintain an erection not only for himself (because failure makes him less of a man) but for his partner, as many women and gay men take any limpness as a personal slight. Indeed, many men think an erection equals desire, even though they can wake up with an erection (caused by the pressure of the bladder on the prostate) or have a fear-induced erection (this is how men have been forced to perform sex acts at gun point).

Conversely, a soft penis does not mean that a man is not excited. For instance, many men will lose their erection while performing oral sex because their attention is directed to their partner, not themselves. As I have said many times in this book, erections come and go. Ultimately, the only thing a lost erection signifies is a lack of blood flow to the penis. This could be caused by various health conditions (diabetes, heart disease, multiple sclerosis, and low testosterone), various medications (antidepressants, beta blockers, sleeping pills, antipsychotics, and some cardiovascular drugs), street drugs (ecstasy, heroine, and in higher doses, cocaine, marijuana, and LSD), long-term cigarette smoking, and alcohol abuse. Additionally, the lack of erection could be due to fatigue or preoccupation with another matter.

When psychologists at Harvard University looked at what 2,250 volunteers were thinking about during a range of pleasurable activities, they discovered that their minds wandered 70 percent of the time. Even when having sex, people only concentrate 90 percent of the time. This figure will drop considerably during times of stress. So although men might still have sexual desire, and certainly have a need to be intimate with their partner, they might not be able to maintain an erection.

"I wanted to prove so much that I could be good at something," said Nicholas, forty-one, "especially after younger and less experienced men started to get promoted over me at work. The more I worried about my work situation, the worse my sex life got. Things with my wife, April, start off fine—I'm erect and ready to penetrate, but if April isn't properly lubricated or I have trouble entering, that's it. My concentration goes, and it's all over. April tries to be nice, but I know she's disappointed. Hell, I'm disappointed. A complete failure."

There was something else troubling Nicholas, but it took a while for him to have enough courage to continue. "I have these images of April with another man and having these orgasms that leave her panting and screaming with pleasure. They really haunt me. I don't think I can keep her if I can't satisfy her."

## How to deal with erectile dysfunction

One of the advantages of Viagra and similar drugs is that what used to be called "impotence" is now freely discussed. The disadvantage is that both men and women are quick to label occasional problems maintaining an erection as erectile dysfunction, which can exacerbate rather than ease the problems. Even many younger men are using such drugs as a sort of "insurance policy." The result is that none of the underlying myths about sex have been challenged, and the problems are medicated rather than solved. So what's the alternative?

- *Listen to your body.* You are not a sex machine, and it could be that your body is trying to tell you something. For example, "I'm angry for being taken for granted" or "This relationship is not working for me" or "I'm burnt out." In many ways, a lack of erection is an early warning that something important needs to be attended to. Certainly Nicholas discovered that half the problems were in his head not his penis. "I was expecting far too much from myself. When I stopped and looked at my workload, the amount that I was drinking, and my anger about my wife's spending, it was not surprising that I wasn't really up for sex."

- *Get a health check.* Speak to your doctor and be certain that you don't have any undiagnosed health problems. If you are on a medication that might be interfering with your sex life, there is probably an alternative prescription. Be aware that most doctors, like the population at large, are often embarrassed about discussing sex and do not routinely ask about the side effects of prescription drugs on erectile function.

- *Be positive.* Celebrate the pleasures of the soft penis, as it is just as sensitive as an erect one. Many men discover that they still enjoy receiving oral sex, and their partners enjoy the sensation of the penis growing and stiffening in their mouth. Even if you don't become fully erect, it is still possible to masturbate or be masturbated to ejaculation. If you have been following my program, you will also be comfortable giving and receiving sensual pleasure with your fingers and tongue. Therefore, losing an erection does not mean that lovemaking has to stop. In fact, many women find it easier to have an orgasm from masturbation or oral sex than intercourse. (There is more about this later in the chapter.)

- *Stop catastrophizing.* Negative statements like "I'm old" or "My wife will leave me" are not only most likely inaccurate but have a magnetic quality to attract other depressing thoughts. Next time your inner voice starts putting you down, instead of listening, imagine taking a baseball bat and knocking the negative statement out of your head. Stop making repeated apologies for your condition, as this will make you feel worse, and it does not make your partner feel better either. In fact, many women just get angrier because, they reason, if you meant the apology you would have gotten help earlier. (Unfortunately, as women are socialized to ask for and give help, they find it difficult to understand how shameful it is for a man to admit to failing at something, especially in this area.)

- *Focus on more positive images.* Instead of anticipating losing your erection, imagine sustaining one and staying calm and using your fingers and tongue to pleasure your partner. Imagine the great sex you're going to have in the future—in detail. Finally, recall your other virtues "great dad" or "sensitive listener."

- *Give yourself time.* If you can step away from the tyranny that sex equals intercourse and become less anxious about your erection, you will discover the truth that erections go, but they also come back. There is no reason why you can't continue to enjoy sex, no matter your age.

## Lack of Ejaculatory Control

One-third of men cannot control when they ejaculate. It is not just younger men, but men in their forties and fifties who reach orgasm too quickly (what is known as premature or rapid ejaculation) or take too long (retarded ejaculation). For the rest, control is never perfect, but up to a point, they can choose when to keep going and when to retreat. When a man has poor control and orgasms quickly—possibly after only a few thrusts—it will make him anxious and miserable. Meanwhile, his partner will often suffer from lack of desire.

As one woman said to me, "Why bother if it's all over before I get warmed up?"

By contrast, men with retarded ejaculation sound like great lovers; after all, they can have intercourse forever. However, regular bouts of thirty, forty, and even sixty minutes can leave both men and women sore and frustrated, especially if he is unable to ejaculate and provide their lovemaking with a sense of completeness. Fortunately, ejaculatory control is the most straightforward problem to solve. All you need is knowledge, attention, and skills, all of which can be taught. First, I will deal with premature ejaculation (PE).

### How to deal with premature ejaculation

Like most sexual problems, PE is best broken down into small steps:

- *Consult your doctor.* Low levels of some antidepressants have been known to slow down men's ejaculatory response and this has led to a range of drugs and creams coming onto the market. Some men would rather do without them, as the side effects can include anxiety, sore mouth, dizziness, and sleep disturbance. The creams aim to numb the penis and are applied about thirty minutes before intercourse and have to be thoroughly wiped away or else they will reduce sensitivity of the vagina. Although not for everyone, there is a place for medication in combination with the following exercises.

- *Listen to your body.* Men with poor ejaculatory control are not focusing enough on the sensations in their own body. It is great to be a considerate lover but not to the point that you ignore the signs of impending ejaculation. So take time out to masturbate alone. The first time there is no need to do anything different from normal; just be aware of the growing sense of arousal and tension. Notice the sensations in your penis when you cross the point of no return—when the seminal vessels and the prostate gland begin to contract and ejaculation is inevitable. This is valuable information for the next step.

- *Practice the Stop-Start Method.* The stop-start method was pioneered in the mid-1950s by Dr. James Semans. While in the first step you masturbated alone to ejaculation (to learn to recognize the signs that you were approaching an orgasm), I want you to stop each time you reach the threshold of climaxing. Quickly breathe out a few times, as this will reduce the tension in your body and your excitement level. Rest for a few seconds, and when you feel under control again, resume masturbation. (Some men without PE call this practice "edging" and use it as a way of prolonging sex.) Try to vary the strokes from slower to faster (and see what effect this has); alternate your grip (two fingers and thumb or whole hand) and where you stimulate (start with the tip and then move farther down the penis). After a few sessions where you have learned to reach the threshold and retreat, add in an extra dimension and masturbate with massage oil or some other form of lubrication. Some men find it helpful to monitor their levels of arousal by using a traffic-light code: green (keep going), yellow (caution/slow down), red (stop). Aim to be able to masturbate for fifteen minutes alone before moving to the next step.

- *Recruit your partner.* Explain to your partner that you will stop whenever you are in danger of reaching the threshold, and that she or he needs to be still too and not thrust up to meet you. The traffic-light system is a quick and easy way of communicating what is happening in your body. The stops will probably need to be a bit longer than when masturbating alone. Take deep breaths, relax, and enjoy the pleasant sensation of being inside his or her body. Some couples will talk to each other or whisper sweet nothings. Try varying your speeds and how far in and out that you thrust, as this is how men with good ejaculatory control delay their orgasms. Accidents are common, but don't worry, it is a chance to practice using your tongue and fingers to satisfy your partner. Solid proof that ejaculation does not mean the end of lovemaking will reduce your anxiety and reassure your partner that his or her needs are not being ignored. In addition, the accident will have provided data for redefining your point of no return and improving control.

- *Give yourself time.* Aim for about fifteen minutes of intercourse before ejaculating. It will probably take a while to reach this point. I recommend men masturbate alone two or three times a week to gain control and then work with their partner at a similar frequency using the start-stop method. Don't fall below twice a week, as sexual frustration will hamper rather than promote control. In total, I would expect a man to take somewhere between four and six weeks to gain ejaculatory control. If this program does not work or you find it hard to follow, there is an alternative approach developed by Masters and Johnson, the founders of sex therapy called the "squeeze technique," which involves squeezing the penis rather than stopping intercourse. A good sex therapist will help explain more and support you through the process.

### How to deal with retarded ejaculation

Although most men will have occasions when they cannot reach a climax through intercourse, there are some who find it difficult to and therefore rarely or never ejaculate in their partner's vagina or anus. Jonathan, thirty-eight, had had many partners over his sexual career. "It doesn't matter what I do, for how long or how attractive I find the girl, I never can ejaculate inside her. Some of the lovemaking has been very passionate, and I've sort of stopped worrying. When I know she's satisfied, I stop. There have been times when I've faked it, but these days I can't see the point."

Retarded ejaculation is more an emotional problem than a physical one, and I was not surprised to learn that Jonathan had problems letting people get emotionally close, and none of his relationships had lasted for more than a few months. "I can't stand feeling obligated; it's like the walls are closing in on me, and I go all quiet. She'll start pushing for answers, which makes things worse, and one of us, normally me, will call it quits."

When I started working with Jonathan, he had recently gotten out of a short relationship where there had been a strong mutual sexual attraction. "Right at the beginning, she'd said she didn't see us having a future," he explained, "and that sort of let me off the hook and I could relax and really enjoy the sex." With this woman, Jonathan had "finished myself off" by masturbating after he withdrew. Up to that moment, he had only masturbated to ejaculation in private.

The main focus of our work was combating Jonathan's anxiety at the beginning of relationships (by helping him to talk about his fears rather than suppress them). When one of his dates turned into a relationship, we decided to work on the retarded ejaculation too. "We'd made love a few times and when I pulled out, she asked, 'don't you want to climax?' so I masturbated myself and she held my other hand. It was really nice," explained Jonathan. Over the next few weeks, I encouraged Jonathan to ask his girlfriend to straddle across him so he could fondle her breasts or kiss her as he masturbated. The next stage, he would masturbate himself and penetrate her after he'd passed the point of no return and then climax inside her.

"To be honest, the pleasure isn't much greater for me, but she enjoys it and we feel closer cuddling afterward."

Over time, Jonathan started to relax enough to let go emotionally and reach a climax without masturbating. His retarded ejaculation was something that belonged in the past.

If you suffer from retarded ejaculation, it is important to discuss the problem with your partner rather than faking an orgasm or hoping the problem will go away. In my experience, your wife or girlfriend will be relieved that you have given her permission to talk about the problem. You will also be able to reassure her that it is not an issue she should take personally (as she will be worried that you cannot ejaculate because she's not attractive or good enough). It could be this talk alone relaxes both of you enough to resolve the difficulty. Alternatively, try withdrawing, masturbating yourself (or let your partner pleasure you), and finishing off in her vagina.

If you're single, I would recommend seeking emotional help, especially if you find it hard to trust and fully let yourself go in a relationship. Too often, men will embark on a new relationship, hoping for the best, but wind up reinforcing their fear of being unable to reach a climax.

## FEMALE-SPECIFIC
## SEXUAL DIFFICULTIES

As I've already discussed, I believe that when a couple is having sexual problems it is a shared problem that happens to be exhibited by one person. If you have turned directly to this section, please look through the section on male-specific sexual difficulties to understand how these, along with a lack of knowledge, communication, and adequate technique, can feed into female-specific issues.

Parents, school, media, and the wider society send girls even more complicated messages than they do boys. On one hand, daughters are encouraged to excel, get good grades, be independent, forge a successful career, and "have it all," but on the other hand, the old-fashioned idea that a woman is pathetic or pitiable if without a man is still a pervasive one. In the same way that a weak man is somehow not a man, a woman without a husband or children is somehow less feminine. While men are competitive on the sports field and in finances, women compete for attractiveness and having the most successful, well-adjusted, revered children. At least men are partially in control of their arena, i.e., they can practice their athletic skills or study business books. Women, however, are competing in an arena that is largely outside their control, like slowing down aging and raising successful children.

While sex is a simple source of pleasure for boys, sex for girls is a minefield. "I was only twelve years old and my dad had given me money to buy a dress for a party he was giving," explains Julia, who is now thirty. "I just thought it was pretty, but it must have been too short and revealing because I remember the looks on all the men's faces when I walked in the room. It was exhilarating and a nice change from feeling ignored and powerless after my parents divorced.

"My newfound attractiveness was also frightening," she explained. "My uncle cornered me in the kitchen and told me I was 'jail bait.'" Before too long, Julia's sexuality became a battlefield between her and her mother. She lost her virginity at fourteen, and when her mother discovered that Julia was on the pill, she threatened to report Julia to the police for underage sex unless she broke up with her boyfriend (who was a year older). However, if a boy was discovered to be having sex at this age, many fathers would congratulate him.

When you consider the anxiety and confusion that conflicting messages about sex puts upon girls and their sexuality—a sexy woman has power over a man, but don't you dare use it, or else risk being a slut or "jail bait"—and add to the recipe the myths girls are taught about sex, it is no wonder sexual issues arise even years later in relationships.

So what are the myths about sex and women?

- Women are not as interested in sex as men and don't have the same sexual urges.
- To want sex is slutty.
- Good girls don't.
- Bigger breasts are more feminine.
- Vaginas are dirty.
- Women should please men in bed.
- While men have an on-off switch, women have hundreds of dials that all have to be at the right place.

In my experience, a woman's level of comfort with her sexuality is directly related to how her mother felt about her own. "My mother had an unrelenting 'abstinence only' sex-education policy, which in retrospect, I think was very damaging. However, I could never confront her about it because I knew I'd upset her," wrote Stella on my website, who despite being thirty-three has only had one casual and short-lived relationship.

Stella continued, "When I was a teenager my mom was always pointing out that sex outside marriage was wrong. I can't stress how strong the message was, how it stayed with me, and how I now feel very scared of sex. After I left home at eighteen, I was extremely shocked that other people my own age were having sex, and their parents didn't mind! These days I don't believe that sex outside marriage is wrong, but I can't get my mother's judgment out of my head."

While boys handle their penises on a daily basis (when urinating), girls are not encouraged to look at their vaginas. Ultimately, if a mother is not at peace with her genitals, it is unlikely that her daughter will be comfortable exploring her own vagina, discovering her clitoris and the pleasures involved. When I have suggested to some female clients that they could take a hand mirror and look at their genitals, I might as well have suggested that they dance naked through the aisles of their local supermarket. Ultimately, for these women, it is okay for their husband to explore their vagina with his tongue or fingers but not for them to know their own way around. It is hard to think of anything sadder than someone else being allowed to receive pleasure from your body, but denying it yourself.

> *"While boys handle their penises on a daily basis (when urinating), girls are not encouraged to look at their vaginas."*

With so many unfortunate myths and mixed messages about sex, it is not surprising that some women find it hard to relax and that their bodies refuse to cooperate.

## Female Anorgasmia

According to the National Survey of Sexual Health and Behavior in Great Britain, 85 percent of men report that in their last sexual encounter their partners achieved orgasm. When women were asked the same question, only 64 percent said that they achieved orgasm. Why is there such an orgasm gap? I'm afraid that we're back to that myth that is undermining good lovemaking: sex equals intercourse. While men are likelier to orgasm when sex includes vaginal intercourse, women are likelier to orgasm when a variety of sexual acts are included (like masturbation and oral sex). Unfortunately, this basic fact is not widely known. Throw in a lack of knowledge about women's genitals on the parts of both women and men, and we have a lot of unhappy women unfairly labeled as "sexually dysfunctional."

Anorgasmia is when someone, male or female, cannot achieve an orgasm. Sometimes anorgasmia stems from a medical issue (diabetes, multiple sclerosis, or some pelvic trauma from falling on a ladder or gymnastics beam), a side effect of drugs (antidepressants and selective serotonin reuptake inhibitors or heroin addiction), but most commonly the problem is a combination of a woman's lack of knowledge about her vagina and her partner's technique.

The clitoris has more nerve endings than any other structure in the human body, somewhere between six and eight thousand, which is four times as many nerve endings as the penis has. Not surprisingly, the clitoris provides the most intense pleasure. Unfortunately, the clitoris rarely gets stimulated during sexual intercourse. Sometimes the penis entering and withdrawing the vagina tugs at the vaginal lips, which are attached to the clitoral hood and provides indirect stimulation. The clitoris can also be stimulated by a woman rubbing against a man's pelvis, especially when the woman is on top and leaning forward enough. However, it is difficult to maintain contact in this manner during intercourse. The advice from sex therapists is to use fingers. Ultimately, it is not important whether a woman reaches a climax through intercourse alone, intercourse and masturbation combined, or through oral sex or masturbation. There is simply no hierarchy of orgasm. What counts is that she feels good and the couple feels close and satisfied.

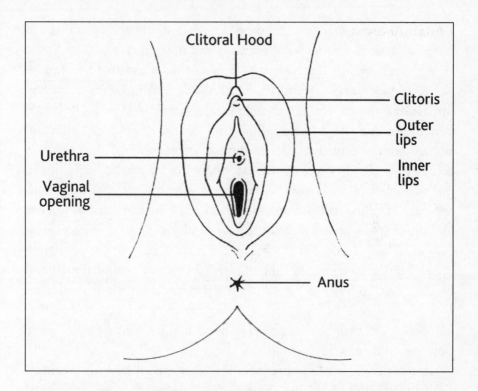

When I quiz couples about their sex lives and ask if the woman has an orgasm, there is often confusion. While male ejaculation is obvious, a woman's climax is largely invisible. So how do you know if you've had one or not? The best way to describe the experience is that an orgasm is a bit like a sneeze—a buildup of tension and then a release. In most cases, when I offer this explanation, a woman will relax and nod. Yes, she has had an orgasm. Unfortunately, all the clichés of romantic novels—where the description of a quivering body or heaven and earth moving—can lead some women to question the response in their own bodies.

There is also as much misinformation about vaginal lubrication as there is about male erection. During lovemaking, blood flows to the vagina and causes it to expand and lengthen while the vaginal lips puff up. Some people think a lack of lubrication means less desire or interest in sex, but some women simply lubricate more than others. There are also times in a woman's menstrual cycle when secretions can be minimal, regardless of how turned on she is. Having recently given birth or nursing a baby will also reduce the amount of lubrication. Other factors that can reduce secretions are some cold remedies and street drugs.

Although women can achieve an orgasm through vaginal penetration alone, the best way is to stimulate the clitoris by rubbing lightly in rocking or circular motions. The lighter and more lubricated the touch, the better. While men don't need further stimulation past their point of no return, women require consistent and continued attention until the orgasm is complete or else they will not climax. Some woman can be very still and quiet just before an orgasm, almost as if listening and waiting for its approach. Unfortunately, many men think their partner has lost interest and stop, thereby aborting the orgasm. The advice to men from sex therapists is to keep going and for women to mentally accept the oncoming orgasm. Prior to climaxing, the clitoris can retreat behind the clitoral hood. Don't go looking for it, just keep stimulating the general area. Communication is very important at this point as every woman is different. Some like their partners to slow down and be a little gentler while others want them to keep going.

In most cases, where women fear that they cannot have an orgasm, I find that offering knowledge, helping their partner improve his ejaculatory control (so intercourse lasts longer), or introducing other forms of lovemaking beyond intercourse resolve the problem. If this does not work, I suggest getting your doctor to refer you to a sex therapist.

More commonly, I see women who do have orgasms but only occasionally. A typical example is Carol, in her midfifties, who has been married for over thirty years to Declan, fifty-nine. "I always say that sex, for me, is not about having an orgasm because I enjoy the closeness and I like giving Declan pleasure, but sometimes I do wonder, *What about me?*"

In the early part of their marriage, Carol had achieved orgasm through intercourse but not in the past twenty years. "Something changed. I don't know what," she explained. Fortunately, she had recently started reading self-help books and gained a better understanding of her body. When Declan's job took him abroad for three months at a time, she bought a vibrator and found that it reliably gave her an orgasm. Although they used the vibrator together, it did not become a regular part of their lovemaking.

When we reached the Two Weeks of Variety in my program, Declan shadowed the way Carol played with her genitals but was unable to give her an orgasm. When I questioned them further, I discovered that there were three problems. The first being that Carol felt she *had* to orgasm to complete the exercise.

"What I've liked about the previous exercises is that there is no planned destination," she said.

I reassured her that there was no requirement to orgasm, but as we talked more, it became clear that being unable to give Carol an orgasm was a source of sadness for Declan.

"I'm worried that I might hurt her, so I think I'm too tentative," he explained.

"So what do you think is the difference between the vibrator and Declan's fingers?" I asked.

Fortunately, Carol had been pondering this question on her own and already knew the answer. "The vibrator covers a greater area and provides greater pressure. Also with the vibrator, I'm not worried about wearing Declan out."

"How long did he masturbate you for?" I asked.

"About five minutes," she replied.

I looked at both of them quizzically.

Carol laughed. "Yes, I suppose a penis can wear out in five minutes but not fingers."

When we had looked at their preferred types of lovemaking (and did the questionnaire together), Carol was surprised to discover that she enjoyed trance.

"It takes time to fall into trance; certainly more than five minutes," I explained, "and repetitive patterning is important. By this, I mean making the same type of move over and over, perhaps varying the pressure."

As we talked more about masturbation, it became clear that Carol enjoyed plenty of different types of touching in the first stages, but as the orgasm approached and she fell into a trance, switching to patterning was preferred. For Declan to achieve the same effects as the vibrator, he would experiment with using two or three fingers during the variety phase of masturbating. To achieve more pressure, Declan would explore different depths of penetration (although Carol could use her hand to encourage him to push down harder or lift his fingers back if his touch was too firm). I also encouraged him to be much closer when he watched her masturbate at the beginning of the exercise, so he could truly see and understand her technique.

To keep the exercise balanced, I wondered if Declan would enjoy more variety of touch (different grips and speeds) when Carol masturbated him. In this way, she could torment him by stopping and starting and not giving him the patterned touch, which prompts ejaculation, until she chose the moment.

The next week, they were happy to report that not only had Declan given Carol an orgasm but by delaying Declan's orgasm, and really "torturing" him, she had taken his enjoyment of sex to a new level too.

If you sometimes find it hard to reach orgasm, please talk to your partner rather than fake an orgasm or pretend that it's not important for you to climax. I would also consider experimenting together with different sex toys as with these it's easier to control the speed and type of stimulation. Most men find the idea of vibrators exciting and a way of spicing up lovemaking. If you're concerned that he will think you're "replacing" him, you could offer to run the vibrator gently over the underside of his penis and scrotum or masturbate him, holding it parallel with his penis. In this way, he will see that you can both enjoy these toys and that neither of you has been substituted.

Show your partner how you like to masturbate yourself and encourage him to get down close so he can see what kind of stimulation you enjoy. When it's his turn to take over, encourage him to keep going, even if you've gone quiet, as this might be the moment when you reach the threshold.

If all this seems difficult, I find it helps to recast this as a game where you are *both* trying different ways of stimulating each other. For example, while he is trying different pressures, places, and ways of touching, you can experiment by varying how you masturbate his penis (two forefingers above and thumb below or whole-hand grip), where (over the head or at the base), and at what speeds.

## Vaginismus

This is the technical term for a woman's inability to engage in any form of vaginal penetration, not just sexual intercourse. Some women cannot insert a tampon nor have a full gynecological examination. A bit like the reflex of blinking when something approaches your eye, the vagina contracts and penetration is painful or impossible. In most cases, the problem is psychological, but it is worth checking for infection, which might be causing irritation or inflammation.

Vaginismus is most likely to affect young women in their teens and twenties, although some wait many years before seeking help. It is caused by the usual combination of problems: lack of knowledge, the myth that sex equals intercourse, and poor male technique.

*Lack of knowledge.* Although we think of the vagina as a hole, it is more a potential space than a real one. When unaroused, the vaginal walls are relaxed and touch each other. However, when the vagina is sexually excited, the walls expand and can easily accommodate a penis.

*Poor male technique.* Unfortunately, an inexperienced man (often one worried that he will not be able to sustain his erection) will blunder toward the vagina, not giving his partner enough time to relax and become aroused. Not surprisingly, his partner will tense up, and so will her vagina.

*Unhelpful myths.* Many people believe sex equals intercourse, so instead of trying other forms of lovemaking like oral sex to relax the vagina, the couple will decide to abandon sex altogether after a few painful prods of the penis.

*The result.* Normally, the woman feels shame and the man is angry, thereby increasing the anxiety levels the next time the couple makes love. Anxiety and tension make vaginismus worse and turns the problem from a temporary setback into an impenetrable wall between the couple.

When Carrie was seventeen and in her first relationship (with a boy the same age), they had nowhere to go to make love. "We had a couple of attempts on my parents' sofa, but I was always worried they would come home, and his parents never went out," she explained.

Carrie's mother had never discussed sex. Although her mother was not explicitly "anti-sex," she found any discussion of emotions uncomfortable, so discussing something as personal as her daughter's body or giving her permission to explore it was simply impossible. "I don't know if it was fear, anxiety, or what, but that first time I just couldn't relax enough for him to enter me," said Carrie. "But the weirdest part is that my boyfriend and I didn't talk about it. He just put himself away and that was that. We tried a couple more times, but it was no better."

Carrie went on to have two more relationships that were sexual but involved no penetrative sex. At twenty-six, she married an old university friend. "We talked about having a baby, which was strange, because goodness knows how that was going to happen, but we never discussed my problem. He was a nice guy, who put me on a pedestal, but I had no respect for him."

It was not until Carrie was thirty-one and divorced that she started a short relationship that turned out to be incredibly sexual. "I don't know if it was because I was older and more confident, the overwhelming attraction I felt for him, or that he was more experienced and knew how to turn me on, but I had no problem at all. Sex was a revelation. I finally understood what everybody was talking about."

Unfortunately, this boyfriend moved abroad and the relationship ended. It was not until Carrie had a series of sexually rewarding, but emotionally empty, relationships that she talked to anyone about her history of vaginismus. It turned out that Carrie had a fear of intimacy—baggage from her repressed childhood. We also worked on destroying the myth that nice girls don't enjoy sex. Halfway through her counseling, she met a man who she both respected and wanted to go to bed with, who became her boyfriend. Fortunately, she had gained enough confidence to discuss her fears with him. "We took things really slowly. Lots of kisses, cuddles, and stroking until I was almost begging him to penetrate me."

If you are in a long-term relationship and find intercourse painful or impossible, sex therapists have techniques to help. This includes the touching exercises in this book, which help you and your partner talk more openly about sex, as well as experimenting with a series of dilators. As the word "dilate" suggests, dilators are a series of tampon-shaped implements that start small and grow in girth until they are similar to the average-sized penis.

## SEXUAL PROBLEMS
## ARE SHARED PROBLEMS

As I've already explained, people are quick to label themselves as having "a problem," despite sexual difficulties having roots in a variety of over-lapping places. Hopefully, now that I've discussed the male- and female-specific sexual issues, you will accept my premise that these are *shared* problems even though one person might be exhibiting it. Taking Carrie and her vaginismus as an example, how much of the dysfunction was due to her inability to relax and how much to her early partners' clumsiness and lack of knowledge? Frequently, sex therapists discover that a woman might come to therapy with anorgasmia, but her partner has poor ejaculatory control. I saw a couple in which the man had retarded ejaculation but his wife had a disgust of semen. If he came close to climaxing through masturbation, she swathed his penis in tissues. Unsurprisingly, he would quickly lose interest.

Determining who has the sexual problem is a bit like the old philosophical debate: which came first the chicken or the egg? Ultimately, it does not matter who exhibits the problem. It is the relationship as a whole, not one half that needs help. Taking away the idea of "blame" makes it easier to work together as a team and improve lovemaking. And the good news is that the specific sexual problems outlined in this chapter are easy to treat and the success rates are high. If you have been following my weekly exercises, you will have a good foundation from which to work on resolving these difficulties. If you are still having problems, your doctor will be able to refer you to a specialist sex therapist.

## SOMETHING TO SLEEP ON

**In summary, remember:**

- When one of you has a low level of desire, it is easy to think there is something wrong with you or your partner. However, sex is complex and the answers are seldom as simple as that.

- The way that men and women have been socialized (and to a lesser extent our biology) leads to different approaches to sex, which makes it harder to understand each other's viewpoint and creates a barrier to good lovemaking.

- Most sexual problems have their roots in the myth that sex must include intercourse.

- Ultimately, all it takes to have a better sex life is knowledge and a vocabulary to discuss what turns you on with your partner—two things that I hope this book has given you.

# SEX ED

### EXERCISE 19    SIMMERING

Many people are so cut off from their sexuality that they miss the everyday triggers for feeling desire. The following exercise will not only help you recognize the sparks but help fan them into flames.

- When you see someone attractive on the street, give yourself permission to enjoy their beauty, the way they move, or how they make you feel. Alternatively, if you prefer, it could be a character in a movie or a celebrity. Don't feel guilty about getting turned on by someone other than your partner. People with good levels of desire naturally allow the inspiration found all around them to help simmer their passion.

- Take a moment out of your day to dream about what you'd like this beautiful person to do to or with you. Picture everything in detail, her hands touching you, his mouth begging to be kissed. Allow the images to form in your head.

- Later, in a quiet moment, bring the images back and watch your private erotic movie again.

- The third time you conjure your image, superimpose your partner's head onto the stranger's body and imagine him or her making love to you. Once again, let the images come to life and the desire build. You are a sexual being and have the right to enjoy these feelings.

- When you greet your partner, allow a frame or a couple of images from your exotic movie to play back in your head. This will guarantee a smile on your face, more than a cold peck on the cheek, and, most important, the warm-up to a good evening together.

- At the end of the week, look back at all the sexual impulses that inspired you and celebrate them. Have there been more than you expected? Had these triggers existed in the past, but you were too unaware to notice them?

## EXERCISE 20    SEXUAL JEOPARDY

If it is difficult to ask your partner's opinions about sex or to initiate a discussion about what you enjoy and how to improve your lovemaking, why not make a game out of it? Write all the questions found below on separate pieces of paper, fold them up, and put them in a hat. Toss a coin to see who picks and asks a question first. After the other person has answered, the questioner gives his or her opinion. Take turns. For the yes/no questions, there are supplementary questions: "Why? What? Tell me more."

*What is the one thing you've never been able to tell me about sex?*

*How does your mood impact our lovemaking?*

How important is romance in lovemaking?

In your opinion, what is the difference between having sex and making love?

Do you think role-playing during sex is interesting?

What are you embarrassed to ask for during sex?

What do you think of your body?

Which part of my body do you like the most?

Do you think our sex life has enough variety?

What is the most important part of lovemaking to you?

What do you think foreplay should consist of?

What do you wish I would do more of?

What do you wish I would do less of?

Why do you fall asleep/want to talk after sex?

Do you like oral sex?

Do we have sex enough?

Complete this sentence: I really like it when you . . .

Do you have a fantasy you want to act out?

How can I show you that I want sex?

Is there anything about sex that makes you uncomfortable?

Would sex toys improve our lovemaking?

Do we need to change the places in which we make love? (Either location or the general environment?)

How can we make sex better?

After you have finished answering a question each, discuss what you have discovered about each other and how you could incorporate this information into your lovemaking, either as a treat or as part of your regular repertoire.

# Chapter Nine

# Affairs and Sex Abuse—
# More Culprits That Put Out the Fire

When it comes to resolving sexual difficulties, it is really important that you and your partner work as a team, but what happens when his or her behavior is making you angry or the problem is so complex, and you feel so helpless, that you don't know how to help? In this final chapter, I'm going to look at the three most common problems that divide couples and explain how you can still turn your love life around and put the spark back into your relationship.

## SEX AND THE AFTERMATH OF AN AFFAIR

In the largest survey of its kind, "Sex in America," one in three women and one in seven men reported that they have little interest in lovemaking. On one hand, that's fine. Nobody should have sex they don't want. However, being in a low-sex or no-sex marriage has consequences. In sex therapy, low sex is defined by making love every other week and no sex as less than ten times a year. What about the desires and rights of their partners? Because nobody should do without the sex that they *do* want.

The result is often an unspoken fight between the person who wants little or no sex and the person who would like to have more sex. Typically, the person who wants little or no sex wants his or her partner not only to accept his or her choice but to remain loving, generous, and committed to the relationship. Meanwhile, the person who wants sex also wants to be in a loving and committed relationship, therefore having two choices:

keep asking for sex (which can easily seem like pestering and create a bad atmosphere) or hope that her desire goes away (which is unlikely).

Unfortunately, most couples in this dilemma do not ask for help. (It is hard enough to admit to each other that they have a problem, let alone speak to a third party.) Instead, they stumble along, hoping the issue will solve itself. Maybe a romantic vacation will do the trick or when the children get a bit older, they will have time for each other again. In the meantime, the partner wanting sex is increasingly vulnerable to having an affair or joining an adult dating site (in the hope that he or she can stay married but have casual sex on the side). Although someone embarking on an affair or arranging a sexual liaison doesn't expect to be discovered, it is inevitable. Modern technology facilitates infidelity and leaves a digital trail of emails, texts, credit card bills, and search histories.

Luckily, there is an upside to an uncovered affair, which is just as well considering the pain, heartache, and guilt involved. So what is this positive? It is no longer possible to ignore the underlying sexual issues, and, sometimes for the first time in their relationship, couples begin to talk and resolve their differences.

## THE JOURNEY FROM DISCOVERY TO RECOVERY

It is possible to emerge from an affair with a stronger and better relationship (as I write in my book *How Can I Ever Trust You Again?*). However, there are two types of couples who find it hard to reach recovery. The first are those in long-term low- or no-sex relationships (rather than in one of the temporary lulls in sexual activity that all couples go through because of stress, money worries, or small children). The second are those who get stuck somewhere along the recovery process. The root of their problem might not necessarily be sex, but I've had quite a lot of success treating these couples by looking at their problems through a sexual lens.

The journey from discovery to recovery involves seven steps: Shock and Disbelief, Intense Questioning, Decision Times, Hope, Attempted Normality, Despair (Bodies Float to the Surface), and Intense Learning. So how could improving your sex life speed this process?

## Shock and Disbelief

After ten years of marriage, Suzanne's husband, Josh, told her he didn't feel that he loved her anymore and put most of the blame on their poor sex life. "This had been an issue since we married when my husband lost interest, excluding vacations when things are great," Suzanne explained at our first session. "I tried to explore the matter with him without success on numerous occasions and got to a position where I ultimately accepted that he had a very low sex drive and that I should love him regardless. I felt my husband had similarly accepted my flaws. I was aware that we were having a difficult time, no more so than previous times and we had a special trip coming up that I hoped would help us reconnect."

Suzanne went into shock when her husband asked for "space" and a few days later told her their marriage had "run its course" and subsequently moved out.

## Intense Questioning

After a few days, and sometimes a few weeks, the shock and numbness begins to wear off and is replaced by questions. In the case of Suzanne and Josh, I'd been suspicious when Josh had refused to attend counseling. Apparently, he was "too angry" and "there wasn't any point." In my experience, most people who fall out of love or have become best friends rather than partners, like Josh claimed, are happy to come to counseling either as a favor to their partner or as a way of easing themselves gracefully out of the relationship.

When Suzanne started asking, "how," "when," "why," Josh's answers became increasingly evasive. Finally, she hacked into his email account. "I'd had concerns about him being overly friendly with a woman on a networking site and I found all these explicit messages to her. It was heartbreaking."

At this point in the journey from discovery to recovery, there is a lot of blame flying around. Suzanne blamed Josh for ruining their marriage with someone "he has only known for two minutes," and Josh blamed Suzanne for being angry and distant. No wonder Suzanne felt "our whole relationship seems like a lie" because in many ways it had been built on two lies: "everything is okay" and "it doesn't matter that we're not only having no sex, but we're not talking about it either."

As tempting as it might be to get sucked into the blame game, it is better to step back and ask yourself why your relationship was so vulnerable (to the point that it could be undermined by a few emails) and what changes would you like to make to your relationship, and, in particular, your sex life?

Talking about sex is vital at this stage in the recovery process. First, it challenges your partner's preconceptions about your attitude toward sex. When Duncan, forty-nine, was found out by an explicit text message, he was shocked by his wife's anger. "I honestly thought my wife, Elizabeth, wouldn't mind. She wasn't really interested in sex. It was something she did for me rather than for herself, but I discovered that I'd gotten her all wrong."

Duncan's affair was a turning point for Elizabeth. She reevaluated her relationship and with counseling changed the face she presented to the world. "I was always cool, calm, and in control. If you didn't like it, that was your problem, not mine," Elizabeth explained. "So Duncan's thinking I wouldn't care about him cheating on me with this other woman stopped me. Of course I minded. I minded a lot, but how was he going to know if I kept my feelings to myself? The truth was I enjoy sex, but I can't just turn myself on, the way Duncan can."

Immediately, the problem had changed from Elizabeth doesn't like sex (which seemed an insurmountable obstacle) to Elizabeth takes longer to be turned on (which is easily fixed). Second, talking about sex demonstrates that you recognize that your relationship is in trouble and that something needs to be done.

Tina, forty-one, came to see me as a last resort. Six months previous, her husband, Bob, told her that he had no more love to give and wanted a temporary separation. Tina thought he was having a midlife crisis or a breakdown, as he had a high-powered, stressful job. "He's either withdrawn, angry, or accuses me of not supporting him, which couldn't be further from the truth. I've always been very proud of his success," said Tina.

Although Tina did everything she could to discourage him, Bob took an apartment in town during the week and came back home on weekends to see Tina and their two children. Before long, Tina discovered Bob had joined a dating site and was seeing other women. During our first session, Tina told me everything about his job, his mother, their children, their special bond. However, there was one subject missing: sex. So, finally, I interrupted her and asked about sex. She explained that their sex life had taken a terrible downturn after a car accident caused Bob to be temporarily impotent and over time had dwindled to virtually nothing.

"Why do you think that's important?" she asked.

"What do you think it must be like to be a forty-year-old man who thinks he'll never have sex again?"

"It's not so hot being a forty-something woman either."

"You need to tell him that you want a better sex life too," I told her.

At our next session, Tina reported, "I left last time determined to bring up the topic of sex, but there never seemed to be the right moment. It was tough, but I told him that I too was dissatisfied with our sex life and wanted something better. The look on his face was priceless."

Nothing that Tina previously said against getting a divorce had had the slightest impact on Bob. However, after they talked more about their mutual disappointment over their sex life, Bob put their divorce on hold, and they came for counseling together. (For more advice on talking about sex, see "Sexual Jeopardy" in the exercise section of Chapter Eight for prompts.)

**Decision Time**

Once the majority of the facts about an affair have been discovered, it is time to assess the damage to your relationship and determine your options. There are eight types of affairs, and the chance of rescuing your relationship is largely dependent on which kind of an affair your partner has had. So let's look at these different types and what underlying sexual problems they might reveal.

1. *Accidental.* When discovered, these people claim not to have been

looking for an affair but a friendship had crossed the line. The "friends" bonded by sharing inappropriate details about their relationships, and, in particular, the state of their marital sex lives. Sometimes the betrayal stops short of becoming physical, but either way, it is deeply hurtful and should be taken seriously. An accidental affair suggests that your sex life has been going through a bad patch, for example, the birth of a child, loss of a job, or death of a parent, rather than serious long-term problems.

2. *Cry for help.* These people are quickly discovered because they leave clues lying around or because they confess. These affairs are casual, short-lived, and "didn't mean anything." A cry-for-help affair suggests that something is wrong with your sex life, but there is still time to head it off before the problem becomes serious.

3. *Self-medication.* These people are unhappy or verging on depressed and probably have been for several years, so only the boost of being adored or the excitement of infidelity can compensate for low self-esteem or keep life on a reasonably even keel. A self-medication affair suggests a long-term ingrained sex problem, most probably low or no sex. Alternatively, the sex might be regular, functional, but deeply dull.

4. *Tripod.* These affairs are long-term, committed, and the discovered has talked about leaving his or her official partner. This is the classic triangle of a husband, wife, and mistress, or a woman "torn between two lovers." At the center of the tripod is someone who finds intimacy difficult, so he or she "spreads" the load, normally by having a friendly, largely sexless relationship with their long-term partner and a passionate one with their affair partner. The task is to be sexual and intimate with the same person rather than splitting them into Madonna and whore or nice guy and stud. Unfortunately, to the person having the affair, leaving his or her partner and setting up home with the lover seems the obvious answer. In my experience, these types of affairs end up with a person turning his or her lover into a friend and becoming passionate with someone new or even embarking on an "affair" with his or her ex.

5. *Don Juan or Donna Juanita.* These people have multiple affairs, often overlapping, or lots of casual sex. It is like they have a huge empty void and need endless sex to fill it up. A Don Juan/Donna Juanita has similar issues with intimacy as in the tripod affair, but instead of having one partner, he or she has many. These people are probably abusing sex to make themselves feel better. So although this might appear to be a sexual problem, it is sometimes an issue of sex addiction.

6. *Exploratory.* Everybody wonders what life might have been like if, for example, they didn't get married at eighteen, had not split from their first love, or made any number of different choices. Some people don't just wonder, they track down their first love, experiment with a same-sex relationship, or have a wild fling. Sometimes, people who have an exploratory affair return to their relationship chastened, but more often, it lights the fuse for something even more damaging. An exploratory affair suggests something is deeply wrong with a relationship and the love life in particular, as many people use this type of affair to experiment with different kinds of sex or to try on a different sexual persona. For example, I've heard justifications like "I wanted to find out if it all still worked" and "I knew there was a passionate woman hidden inside the dutiful wife and mother." Even if the person having an exploratory affair or casual sex does decide to stay in his or her relationship, he or she seldom communicates any newfound sexual needs and starts resenting his or her partner for not fulfilling them.

7. *Retaliatory.* As the name suggests, this affair is about getting revenge on an unfaithful partner by being unfaithful. A retaliatory affair turns a difficult situation into a toxic one and makes it harder for a couple to cooperate and resolve their sexual problems. Sometimes I meet people who have retaliatory sex to make their partner jealous in the hope it will rekindle his or her interest. More often, it is a straightforward desire to prove they are attractive or bolster their flagging self-esteem.

8. *Exit.* Breakups are painful, hard, and deeply unpleasant. Many people will embark on an exit affair to provide a boost to their self-confidence, gain some emotional support, and send their partner a clear

message. An exit affair might seem like the end of the road for a marriage, but these rebound relationships nearly always split up, partly because the new partners find it hard to trust each other (after all, the relationship was built on deceit), but mainly because once the dust has settled, they often have little in common. However, there is an exception. Exit affairs with childhood sweethearts or past lovers tend to be more durable. If your relationship crumbled through low-sex or no-sex issues, tell your partner about the sort of sex life you'd like and show him or her this book.

## Hope

Once couples have recovered from the initial trauma of discovering infidelity, or being discovered, and have taken stock of their relationship, many will decide to try again. With the flood of relief and the hope that things can be better comes a boost to their sex life. "It felt really primeval," says June, sixty-one, "like I was reclaiming my man. It was passionate, needy, and a little dark."

Her husband, Trevor, sixty, added, "It was totally unexpected. June was doing things that she's hardly done before, like oral sex. It was a real roller coaster."

Instead of occasional or predictable sex, lovemaking during the hope stage is plentiful and adventurous. Unfortunately, relief can easily tip over into something quite dark with the discovering partner becoming obsessed with details of the sexual transgressions.

Bertie had been married for sixteen years and had two adolescent children when his wife admitted to a "fumble" with a colleague. At first, he was relieved that she broke off the affair and found another job. Unfortunately, he would get flashbacks while they had sex. *She did this sexual act with him. This is what he must have seen.*

## Attempted Normality

It might seem the majority of the problems are all in the past; however, the discoverer of infidelity is still having bouts of despair or depression, and the partner who was discovered is feeling guilty and monitored. Sadly, instead of talking, many couples keep their misgivings to themselves and plough on regardless. So while on the surface, everything seems normal, underneath there are still unresolved issues.

For many couples, the initial burst of "make-up" sex has diminished and the affair partner is still a presence, albeit metaphorically, in their bedroom. "I found myself trying to compete and be better than her, behaving like someone in those porn films," said June. "I hate myself, but I can't stop."

Trevor felt under pressure to perform too. "There was one time, when I was tired, that I couldn't stay hard and June got all upset."

June looked up from her pile of tissues. "That's not how you were with her."

If these issues are not addressed, each party will withdraw to their sides of the bed and begin to believe their sexual problems are insurmountable. (Fortunately, it wasn't too late for June and Trevor, and there will be more about their journey later in the chapter.)

Sometimes, when taking a sexual history of a couple at the beginning of their counseling, I discover that affairs that have long since ended still cast a shadow. In effect, the couple has been trapped in "attempted normality" for years.

## Despair (Bodies Float to the Surface)

A crisis brings both danger and opportunity, and nowhere in the recovery process are these two outcomes more finely balanced than at this stage.

In most relationships, couples know the underlying problems, i.e., she earns more than him or he has an interfering mother, but they step around them and keep everything nice. While faithful couples agree to differ about long-running issues, couples recovering from affairs are so determined to avoid the possibility of it happening again that they work harder, dig deeper, and bring all the problems up to the surface. In the sexual arena, these can be long-term issues like frequency of lovemaking, pornography, who initiates sex, or dressing up. Generally, both partners are only too aware of the problems but have chosen to ignore them.

The crisis of infidelity, however, can encourage one partner to reveal a secret from their past. These can include physical abuse from previous partners, babies born out of wedlock, abortions, and, in particular, childhood sexual abuse. However painful it is to confront these issues, I am always cautiously optimistic as, at last, there is an opportunity to lay the ghosts to rest.

## Intense Learning

In the "attempted normality" stage, all the problems were hidden or had not been properly addressed. Alternatively, the partner who had been unfaithful might have been holding back important information about the affair. Through "intense learning," both partners are in possession of all the facts and ready to work on their relationship (rather than put patches over the cracks or agree to "try harder").

By the time Heather, fifty-six, got to the bottom of Gareth's infidelity, she discovered two affairs, one more serious than the other. "What I can't understand is how my husband claims that he loved both this other woman and me at the same time," said Heather. It was more than an academic question. With Heather doubting Gareth had been honest about his feelings during the affair, she doubted that he loved her today, and this was making her hold back both sexually and emotionally.

So I asked each of them to think about the ingredients for love. Gareth listed some qualities that could be shared with more than one person at a time: affection, respect, attraction, shared beliefs, mental rapport, physical attraction, joy, respect. He also came up with some that needed to be exclusive: faithfulness, integrity, and trust.

Meanwhile Heather duplicated many of Gareth's words but added: forgiveness, a soft place to land when in trouble, accepting a partner's failings, sexual satisfaction, honesty, and happiness. The first few qualities suggested that she might be further along the healing process than she thought.

From completing this exercise with many clients over the past few years, I would define love as possessing three qualities: *commitment, intimacy,* and *passion.* Drawing on this definition, I challenged Gareth.

"It seems to me that you loved neither Heather nor this other woman. You might have felt passion for your mistress but weren't committed, or else you would have set up a home together. You might have been committed to Heather in a 'paying the bills, eating Sunday lunch with the family' sort of way, but you weren't truly intimate. How can you be if you've been holding back so much?"

One of the triggers for the affair had been Gareth losing his job after twenty years with the same company and the depression that followed. It took him months to access the counseling and job-seeking services that had been part of his severance package.

"You couldn't open up to Heather about how much you were hurting or how betrayed you felt?" I pressed.

Gareth looked down at his shoes.

"You might have told the other woman about that pain, but you weren't truly intimate because you were seeing yet another woman at the same time," Heather pointed out.

Finally, Gareth turned to me and said, "Using your definition of love and even my own, you're right. I wasn't truly in love with either Heather or this other woman."

"However, over the last few weeks, you've told Heather everything."

"About ninety-eight percent, I think," Heather chipped in, "and it's taken two years to get here."

"But," I said, "you've finally laid the basis to be intimate again and your sex life has improved beyond all recognition. It seems to me you're ready to love Heather again."

From this conversation, Heather and Gareth each had a goal for intense learning. For Gareth, how could he demonstrate his commitment? (Especially as he often appeared more committed to the demands of his new job than rebuilding his relationship with Heather.) For Heather, could she ask for what she needed and not settle for second best? (Especially as she considered "sexual satisfaction" an important ingredient for love but had not said anything when Gareth could not bear to be touched by her, during the period where she discovered he was having the affair.)

## OVERCOMING A ROADBLOCK TO RECOVERY

Sometimes when a couple has talked about what happened and feel past the affair but still emotionally stuck, I find it helps to put them through the Month of Sensuality, even if a low- or no-sex situation was not one of the main causes of the affair. There are three ways it can help.

1. *Promote honesty.* When couples put aside achieving orgasm, it frees them up to really enjoy touching, kissing, and holding each other. Instead of foreplay lasting a matter of minutes, couples begin to relax, the defenses are lowered, and something inside clicks into place. Over again, they report feeling closer than they have been in years. With this renewed sense of intimacy, many discovered partners will reveal details about the affair that they previously withheld.

   "It took me a while to reveal the full extent of my infidelity while I was abroad on business," explained Trevor, whom we met earlier in this chapter. "Even when we renewed our vows in front of all our friends and family in the roof garden of a five-star hotel, I held details back because I was frightened that if I told the truth I'd lose June."

   However, the graduated sensual touching exercises opened up a new level of honesty where Trevor felt both close enough to trust June and ready to admit to himself that his secret was maintaining the wall between them. "I told June that there had been two one-night stands as well as the affair," explained Trevor. "I got talking to these women in the hotel bar. I knew deep down they were prostitutes, but I pretended to myself they weren't because it was nice to talk to someone who wasn't a work colleague. Of course, we ended up in my room, and afterward I gave them money."

   Immediately after the confession, June was angry and withdrawn, but once the shock subsided, she had a slightly different take. "I was really glad he told me on his own free will. Beforehand, I'd gotten information from cross-examining him or by pulling it from him. I feel better in myself too. When you know there's something more but your partner keeps denying it, you start to doubt your own judgment. It was driving me crazy."

June did not feel like being touched for a couple of weeks, but they soon returned to the program and their intimacy had a new level of intensity. "I wouldn't wish what I've been through on my worst enemy," said June, "but Trevor's infidelity has made me realize that we were just chugging along and not really communicating properly. However, nowadays, we're not only talking more but having the sort of sex we haven't had in years."

2. *Provide structure.* Many couples find themselves going over the same painful material, sometimes as much as six months after discovery. In some cases, there are still important details to be revealed but more often, the discoverer is depressed, feeling alone, and needs reassurance that the discovered really does care. So the discoverer re-opens the same old discussion partly because talking about his or her pain helps release the feelings, but mainly because after both parties have gotten upset, argued, and made up, he or she hears the comforting words "I'm sorry," "I love you," "I won't do it again," and enjoys a cuddle.

After years of thinking it would be simpler if the discoverer just asked to be held rather than belabor a conversation about details of the infidelity, I began putting stuck couples on this program. I found that each week's exercises—and the talking it promotes afterward—provided a structure that made the discoverer feel as if something was being done to repair the relationship without it seeming as if the issue of the affair had been dropped and made the discovered feel as if the past was not sabotaging a future together.

Even though all the main details of her husband's infidelity had been uncovered twelve months previously, Dee, fifty-eight, was still plagued by the details she knew and questions she couldn't answer. "I wake up at four in the morning and can't get back to sleep, so I'll start writing everything down to get it out of my head. All this time later, I'm still plagued by their 'special relationship' and their 'special attraction' and how they went to bed together only an hour after they first met. It's like a dull toothache that never goes away but flares up into something nasty, biting, and painful."

Her husband, Roland, fifty-seven, explained, "I can leave her with a cup of coffee in bed, bright-eyed and bushy-tailed, but two hours later I'll get a text telling me she wants to pack her bags and run away."

So I asked Dee to read her diaries. Many entries were eight or ten pages long and full of repeated painful details: "She's ten years younger" and "He never had erectile problems and never required lubricant" and "Did he start wearing boxer shorts to please her, even though I'd already asked him to change to something more flattering?"

It was clear that being in Dee's head was both exhausting and depressing. After talking about the diaries, Dee decided that she would change her approach. When a thought popped into her head about the affair, she would try to throw it away instead of planting it, watering it, and letting it grow into a jungle. At the same time, I introduced the Month of Sensuality, so that instead of talking about the affair, they started touching each other. Staying detached to her thoughts while participating in the Month of Sensuality worked. Dee stopped obsessing, the touching prompted discussions about their sexuality together (rather than Roland's with his mistress), and when the occasional thought would not wither and die, it was able to be addressed through constructive conversation.

3. *Set goals.* Many people have affairs either because they have lost hope that their relationship can change or because they feel ignored and sidelined. Although the discoverer wants to believe his or her partner that "things will be better" or "we'll make it work," the fear remains to be "once he or she's got me back, everything will slip back to how it was before." Many couples have made similar pledges before, and nothing fundamentally changed. So why should it this time? Meanwhile, the affair partner is holding on to the prospect of "real" change and a "new start." Whether this will be a change for the better remains to be seen.

So how do you combat inertia from the past and the lure of a new relationship? Lots of discoverers use the stick approach, i.e., chastising the discovered for the potential harm to their children, their finances, and themselves. These arguments are perfectly valid, but it is hardly an inspiring banner to march under. Instead of the stick approach, try offering a carrot. And what better carrot is there than reinventing your sex life? Rather than vague promises to try harder, this program provides concrete steps for moving forward. (There is also more about how to bring lasting change to your relationship in my book *Help Your Partner Say "Yes": Seven Steps to Achieving Better Cooperation and Communication.*)

## DEALING WITH SEXUAL JEALOUSY

Jealousy is a very understandable emotion, particularly after an affair, but it is also incredibly destructive. Bertie, whom we met earlier in this chapter, discovered that rather than a brief sexual fumble, his wife had a four-month affair, and her lover had taken explicit photos of her.

"My wife has been my only sexual partner and to that end I saw her as wholesome. The thought of her sexual exploits makes me physically sick. I find it totally disgusting and that makes it hard to have close contact with her."

Bertie genuinely felt that he could never come to terms with what she had done. So what can be done when you are so jealous that it makes it impossible to heal?

*"Jealousy is a very understandable emotion,
particularly after an affair, but it is also incredibly destructive."*

### Understand the Jealousy

At the heart of jealousy is fear. Someone is going to take something precious from us, and we are not going to be able to cope with pain. In fact, the hurt is so overwhelming that for many people like Bertie, the only option is to withdraw love or leave. They imagine that choosing to end the relationship rather than waiting for their partner to leave somehow lessens the pain. However, after spending twenty-five years helping couples cope with the aftermath of relationship breakup, I would say it makes no difference whether someone leaves or is left. The hurt is equal, and, counter-intuitively, the person who sticks with the relationship,

207

rather than the leaver, normally makes the best long-term recovery. This is because stickers are less likely to jump into a new relationship and make the same mistakes all over again. Ultimately, trying to run away from jealousy does not work. Fortunately, there is an alternative: understanding.

If jealousy is a problem in your relationship, ask yourself: *Why am I so frightened of loss? Why do I think I will not be able to cope? What happened in my childhood that might explain my extreme reactions?*

The next component of jealousy is low self-esteem. Deep inside, Bertie believed that since his wife had the opportunity to compare his lovemaking skills with those of another man, he would automatically be found substandard. However, it is perfectly possible that Bertie's wife would discover that, like most affair sex, it was lustful but empty and that she much preferred the caring and committed lovemaking at home.

If low self-esteem is an issue, ask yourself: *Why do I have such a low opinion of myself? Is there a small voice inside my head putting me down, or do the messages come from other people? How could I challenge these destructive voices and these negative messages?* (There is more help in another of my books: *Learn to Love Yourself Enough: Seven Steps to Improving Your Self-esteem and Your Relationships.*)

## Take a Fresh Look at Your Attitudes

At the heart of a lot of jealousy is the notion that our partner *belongs* to us. The idea is reinforced by marriage ceremonies "do you take this man . . ." and "who gives this woman . . ." and popular songs and movies. However, people are not possessions. We might give ourselves sexually to our partner, but they don't "own" us, because that is a heartbeat away from controlling them, knowing what's best for us, and, in the worst cases, domestic violence. Owning is the opposite of loving.

There was something else lurking behind Bertie's jealousy. He was as much upset by the idea that his "wholesome image" of his wife had been destroyed by what she'd actually done. I can understand his shock. His wife was not like the image that he'd carefully constructed and nurtured over the years. From my therapist's perspective, she's actually become a whole lot more interesting. She had the courage to pose for revealing photos, and she was on the threshold of breaking out of the "nice girl/wife and mother" stereotype and starting to explore her sexuality. Of course, that's terribly frightening as we all like to coral our partners into a safe corner and for them to be just how we imagine, rather than accept their true complexity.

### *"Owning is the opposite of loving."*

During my journalism career, I interviewed many authors and was intrigued to find that most of their families do not read their books (or if they do, do so with great reluctance). I think it is because writing reveals a lot about the writer and many partners are uncomfortable about the distance between how they like to see their partner and the person revealed in the work.

Ultimately, one of the challenges of recovering from infidelity is taking back our cherished but probably one-dimensional view of our partner and updating it with something more multifaceted. However, there is a consolation prize. This sense that we can never truly know our partner and that there is always more to discover promotes intrigue, passion, and a more rewarding sex life.

## Talk About the Flashbacks Away from the Bedroom

It is not necessary to explain every horrible twist of your jealous imagination, but if you say nothing about your jealousy-related behavior and the reasons behind it, your partner can easily draw the wrong conclusions. When Miriam, forty-eight, discovered her husband's affair and some very graphic texts describing their lovemaking, she was consumed by jealousy. "This woman kept going on about what a wonderful kisser he was and how his 'urgent tongue conquered her resistance.' It not only made me feel physically sick but just the thought of him kissing *me* made my flesh crawl. So if he went to kiss me, I'd turn my head."

Unfortunately, Miriam did not explain to her husband how kissing triggered vivid pictures of him with the other woman. Later in counseling, her husband revealed that he had interpreted the lack of kisses as

Miriam finding him disgusting. She quickly clarified that she found the images of the infidelity disgusting, not him, and the atmosphere in the counseling room changed dramatically.

In most cases, I find people have constructed a far worse reason for their partner's coldness than the real one. Explaining triggers for jealous feelings, or what I call "showing where the bodies are buried," will not only clear up any misunderstanding but recruit your partner to be a participant in resolving the problems, instead of the enemy and the source of the pain.

Unfortunately, most couples start to talk about the jealousy in bed after it has ruined a round of lovemaking. This is possibly the worst place and moment to do this because instead of the discussion being informed by rational thought, it is hijacked by emotions like hurt, rejection, and anger. So follow my golden rule and discuss sexual jealousy *away* from the bedroom and never after consuming alcohol.

## Find Good Images to Replace the Bad Ones

Instead of allowing the jealous flashback to take root and sour your day, try replacing it with a positive image. This might be a picture of yourself in a favorite or beautiful place or a happy memory from your relationship. Alternatively, try superimposing the painful or tainted image with something new that belongs to just you and your partner.

Gareth and Heather, whom we met earlier in the chapter, seemed to have recovered their sexual vibrancy until what Heather called "a very loving and generous gesture" brought Gareth's infidelity into their bedroom.

"We'd been making love," she explained, "but Gareth was tired and couldn't sustain his erection. In the past, that would have been it and we'd have stopped, but instead he helped me reach a climax with his fingers. A dark voice inside my head wondered why after all these years he'd done that, but I pushed the idea away and enjoyed the moment."

Unfortunately, the idea that he had learned this trick from his affair partner had taken root and the next morning, during a coffee break from working on the garden together, she asked if this hunch were true. Fortunately, Gareth was straight with Heather and explained that his mistress had often wanted him to make love for a second time, but he had been unable and had instead masturbated her.

So instead of letting masturbation belong to the affair, I suggested they put a twist on this form of lovemaking and reclaim it for themselves by doing something that neither they nor Gareth and his mistress had done before. Ultimately, the answer came out of kissing, cuddling, and sensual touching. "We started fondling each other," explained Gareth, "and it got more and more intense until I was masturbating Heather and she was masturbating me at the same time. Normally we'd have stopped and had intercourse, but it felt so good that we continued and came within about a minute of each other."

They had replaced a bad image with a good one.

## MY PARTNER USES PORNOGRAPHY

Next we move on to the second topic that can put out the fires of desire. Men and women are sexually stimulated by different things. Men are particularly visually orientated and, even in their fantasies, concentrate more on body parts and intercourse. In male monkeys, the level of testosterone is boosted when they see a sexually available female or watch another pair of monkeys copulate.

Meanwhile, brain scans of the human male show more activity in the regions associated with visual processing. The same scans in female brains reveal more activity in the parts of the brain associated with emotion and the retrieval of memories. Therefore, it is not surprising that men and women have different attitudes toward pornography.

Gemma and Mark came into counseling after she caught him looking at Internet pornography. "It's not just that I know he's comparing to me to those horrible women," said Gemma, "but that the images are stuck in his head while he's making love to me. Like some sort of 'spank bank.'"

Mark had also admitted that he often masturbated alone. Gemma felt betrayed by this too. "We have a very active sex life, at least three times a week, so why does he have to sneak off into a corner? If he felt turned on, he could have made love to me." Gemma would have been horrified at another finding of psychotherapist Brett Kahr, whose research into fantasies was discussed in Chapter Seven: 90 percent of men and 86 percent of woman masturbate alone on a regular basis. Gemma, however, claimed that she was not one of the statistics.

The arguments about pornography had escalated, and their sex life had become a battlefield. Mark had agreed not to go online for any reason. "I want to keep the peace and show Gemma that she's what matters to me, but work is really difficult without the Internet because I need to order supplies for my business," said Mark.

"You should have thought about that before looking at filth," replied Gemma. "I think you're addicted to porn."

## IS SEX ADDICTION REAL?

When someone is labeled a "sex addict," we immediately picture a Hollywood star who has had a string of affairs or been caught with a prostitute. However, no matter the excuses used by Tiger Woods or admonitions of David Duchovny, there is no agreed upon medical or legal definition for sex addiction. Additionally, the newly revised DSMV, the leading guide for diagnostics, does not recognize sex addiction. So *can* you be addicted to sex?

Therapists are certainly seeing a growing number of men whose lives have spun out of control because they can't stop visiting prostitutes—even though they have promised their wives they'd do so—or have run up bills of thousands of dollars on adult telephone chat lines or regularly spend the *whole* night watching Internet pornography, despite having to go to work in the morning. It is not just the behavior that is so destructive but the repercussions.

For instance, I worked with a man who missed his brother's funeral because he was having sex with a prostitute, and another who would masturbate seven times a day in the office bathroom. He had been caught once and given an official warning, but despite his job being on the line, he had not stopped. These stories, and countless more, have provided the framework for deciding if someone is abusing sex.

- The behavior is compulsive.

- The behavior interferes with normal living and causes severe stress on family, friends, and work.

- Sex is used to block out feelings, self-medicate, or as a "reward" for getting through something stressful or painful, even though afterward the "addict" feels guilt and disgust. Unfortunately, shame just triggers another visit to a prostitute or a marathon porn session.

- Although someone abusing sex will often stop for a while, they find it hard to maintain abstinence for the long term. In the pre-Internet era, for example, men would throw away their magazines and videos but gradually start collecting again. Today, these men will willingly allow their partner to control the password to the family computer but later go out and buy a secret laptop and set up a private Internet account.

- There is often denial about the full extent of usage and dependency. So when an addict is faced with admitting to how many hours is consumed by his or her addiction or the size of the bill, he or she finds it hard to believe when proof is presented.

Further, there are many myths about sex addiction:

- *It is only men who abuse sex.* I have met women who compulsively cruise adult dating sites, often when drunk, and invite strangers to their home, even though many of their "dates" become verbally abusive and turn violent after having sex.

- *It is fun.* The sex is surprisingly joyless and the regret is not just limited to the morning after. Some men report throwing up before meeting a prostitute but feel "obliged" to go through with the sex after having spent hours choosing and arranging the session.

- *It is linked to a high-sex drive.* This is like saying alcoholics are thirstier than the general population. In many ways, it is not about sex at all but a way of anaesthetizing oneself from pain (even though it will cause more pain and set up even more destructive behavior).

- *It is something that you're saddled with for life.* Although some men have been consuming large amounts of pornography since they were teenagers, for many consumption is associated with a particular stage in their lives, such as their wife becoming pregnant or a promotion. Obviously the longer and more ingrained the habit, the harder it is to cure. Like all addictions, the success of treatment depends on the degree of commitment to change.

## WHAT ARE THE ORIGINS OF SEX ABUSE?

For many men, their relationship with pornography is reasonably healthy. It can be a source of information, like when they are young and inexperienced, and a solace when they are between girlfriends or boyfriends. For young women brought up to believe that watching pornography is hip and liberating, it can provide a distraction when they are feeling anxious or bored and a sense of power that they don't have in real life. In the same way that it's perfectly possible to enjoy a drink without becoming an alcoholic, you can use pornography without becoming a sex addict. However, for some people, their relationship with porn is more complicated.

Shane is in his midforties and discovered his father's collection of top-shelf publications when he was thirteen. "It was like a country boy heading to the big city. All these beautiful girls, all laid on these pages for my pleasure. It was complete sensory overload. I looked down and realized that I'd ejaculated."

It was Shane's first orgasm, and, at the time, he had no idea what his body had just done. "I'd squirrel away one of my father's stack of magazines and look at it at my leisure."

Over time, Shane would spend longer and longer amounts of time flipping through the pages. "I'd be looking for just the right image, but if I found something good after just a few minutes, I wouldn't finish masturbating because that would spoil things. I'd slow down and keep looking. Sometimes an hour or maybe two would go by."

The atmosphere in the house was becoming increasingly fraught and his parents' fights had turned nasty. "My brother and I would sit at the top of the stairs and listen to the insults. One night my mother came up with a sandwich in the middle of the night, which, looking back seems a bit strange since I wasn't hungry. But I ate it anyway. That was one of the better times; most nights we were left to our own devices."

"Did you and your brother support each other?" I asked.

"No, we were both in our own little worlds coping as best as we could."

With no reassurance, no cuddles from either parent, and no opportunity to talk, Shane took refuge and comfort in his father's porn collection. "It gave me a warm, fuzzy feeling," he explained.

During his twenties and thirties, Shane had a string of girlfriends—some more important than others—and his porn use subsided. However, at forty, he ended his most serious relationship to date, and shortly afterward, his mother died. Unable to cope with so much loss, he escaped into porn again. "For a while, I could forget how sad and empty I felt." However, there had been a big change since his childhood: the Internet. While previously, he had to cope with the shame of buying a soft porn magazine at a newsstand or risk being seen by someone he knew coming out of a licensed sex shop, the Internet allowed him anonymity. Not only was there unlimited pornography available twenty-four seven, but the sites he visited were littered with advertisements for prostitutes. "I thought, *My business is going well, I can afford to pay for sex. I need never be alone when I need company.*

"Unfortunately, I had no idea about the etiquette or what to do in a brothel. After I had sex with the first prostitute, who was incredibly beautiful, I just burst into tears. It was like a dam bursting from all that pent-up pain. She must have been kind because we made love again. I didn't know that was against the rules. Of course, I tried to see her again, but that wasn't allowed either."

Over the next five years, Shane began to use prostitutes regularly sometimes as often as three times a week. "There is this moment of intimacy but it's only fleeting, and ultimately when you're standing outside on the street, you know it was all an illusion."

Shane would tell himself that he was harming nobody. "It's not like I had a wife or anybody I was betraying. I was single and accountable only to myself."

Certainly the stakes appeared much lower than for married men whose marriages are put in jeopardy by visiting prostitutes. However, Shane *was* harming himself. While "self-medicating" with prostitutes, he was not dealing with his bereavement and the complicated feelings associated with his mother (who he both loved and felt anger toward) or making new relationships (despite his greatest goal being to get married and have children). Worse still, he was switching off his natural empathy for other people when having sex with prostitutes; otherwise, he would have to consider what it was like for the women to "service" so many men or issues like forced prostitution and human trafficking.

When looking back at his other relationships with women during this period, Shane admitted, "I was thinking with my dick when I was on a date. *When am I going to get sex?* or *How could I persuade her into bed? An expensive meal maybe and back to my place for a night cap and if not intercourse perhaps a hand job.* Sometimes, I'd think, *I don't like her enough for all that effort, all that talking, I could just call and order sex.*"

"How do you think these women felt being pestered for sex?" I asked.

"Not very good," he looked at me bleakly. "If I truly want to settle down and get married, I'm not doing myself any favors."

As we reviewed his recent relationships, a pattern began to emerge. "They always complain that I'm only after sex, and I worry that they're only after my money—after all, why would they want to go out without a forty-something man who's carrying a bit of extra weight—and there's always a bill for college that needs paying or they're behind with their rent."

I was struck by how the sexual/financial transaction of prostitution was mirrored in his dating relationships. "So you both end up feeling used?" I asked.

When Shane realized that his prostitution and pornography habits were not just coping mechanisms for being single, but were the reasons he was staying single, he stopped hiring prostitutes and using pornography. (There is more information about his treatment in the exercise section.)

I have told Shane's story in detail, rather than a more extreme example, because many men will be able to relate to it and because it illustrates the three main contributing factors for sex addiction:

1. *Childhood sexual abuse.* Showing pornography to a minor is illegal, and although Shane's father didn't want him to look at his collection, leaving them somewhere his son could find them is reprehensible (as he was not emotionally mature enough for adult content). Most addicts, however, have suffered something much worse—like being physically violated or having their trust violated.

2. *Trigger circumstances.* The loss of Shane's mother and splitting with his girlfriend turned his manageable but still questionable relationship with pornography into a problem relationship with prostitutes. For many people, triggers can be a serious car accident, marital breakdown, the loss of a job, illness, and so on.

3. *Greater opportunity.* In the same way that crack cocaine has dramatically increased the number of addicts despite their recreational use of other drugs without getting addicted, sex addiction experts are reporting that the Internet, and being only a couple of clicks away from a prostitute, is causing men without the normal underlying factors of childhood abuse or any serious triggers to get into trouble with pornography.

Our attitudes to addiction have undergone a revolution, and we are now likelier to see it as an illness than a character flaw. However, when it comes to sex addiction, our attitudes are lagging. "We're still stuck in the seventies, and although we no longer think of an alcoholic as being a tramp on a park bench, we still picture sex addicts as perverts in dirty raincoats," says Paula Hall, who is a sex and relationship psychotherapist and leads a sex addict recovery group. "The reality is that sex addicts come from all walks of life."

Hall thinks understanding the parallels between the use of alcohol and sex is helpful. "In our culture, we're not generally anti-drink, and we don't think a return to prohibition is the answer. In the same way, we don't have problems with sex, and we don't think abstinence works either. However, while we're more forgiving of alcoholics, we still have a closed mind to sex addiction. While, in reality, our relationship to both these drugs is quite similar."

So what are the parallels? With alcohol, most people are "social" users who enjoy a drink without any problems. Similarly, most people are "social" users of sex. However, in the same way that there are "at-risk" drinkers, who often don't know when or can't stop, there are "at-risk" users of sex who have intercourse with inappropriate people, put their health or job at risk, or spend hours looking at Internet pornography. There are three key questions to decide if you or someone you are close to falls into the category of "at risk."

1. Do you spend eleven hours or more a week looking at pornography? (Doing so exhibits compulsion.)

2. If you can't get access to your chosen form of sexual stimulation, does your mood change? (Indicates self-medication.)

3. Do you become irritable, moody, or feel unwell if you do not have access to your chosen form of sexual stimulation? (Suggests withdrawal symptoms.)

Beyond the "at-risk" category of sex addiction, there are "binge" users, who can go weeks and months without abusing sex but then go off the rails and start indulging in destructive activities. Finally, there are "addicts" who regularly use sex or pornography to regulate their moods and help them cope with stress (even though their usage causes more stress).

## HOW SEX ADDICTION AFFECTS PARTNERS

It goes without saying that it is profoundly upsetting to discover that your partner has been visiting prostitutes, watching large amounts of Internet pornography, or using adult dating services. In some ways, the pain is similar to typical infidelity, except there are several additional blows that cause shock and worry. *Did he or she use a condom and am I at risk for sexually transmitted diseases?* The shame is greater. *What would my friends think? Would anybody understand?* The offending behavior is also harder to understand. *At least with an affair, there is the "excuse" of love or being flattered by attention.* Sex addiction is also more challenging, as it can raise questions about the tastes and sexual interests of the men concerned. Men who abuse pornography and use prostitutes are even likelier to lie or minimize the extent of their behavior, as their shame and shock is also greater and likelier to come out in stages than in typical infidelity.

"It's not like I'm a prude," said Cynthia, thirty-one, after she discovered her husband had been visiting prostitutes again. "If he'd told me what he wanted, we could have talked about it. Except he has to lie, go behind my back, and spend money we don't have."

Her husband, Martin, thirty, was full of remorse.

"I really love her and wouldn't do anything to hurt her," he told me.

"So why do it?" Cynthia asked.

"I have these fantasies; they just build and build until I have to do something about them. Not that anything lives up to what I expect. I promise myself I'll never do it again, but a new fantasy, a new sexual peak, looms and I just have to go after it."

After the most recent transgression, Cynthia had started compulsively checking the computer and bank statements, and phoning to ensure Martin was where he said he would be. Other common reactions to someone discovering a partner is abusing sex include:

- Reawakening of old wounds in the relationship. (Cynthia and Martin's battles over spending money came back to the surface.)

- Triggering a partner's past traumas. (These can be everything from childhood sexual abuse to something completely disassociated with sex, like bereavement or a car accident.)

- Damaging the sex life of the couple. (Cynthia felt too disgusted to be sexually intimate with Martin, and he felt too ashamed to ask.)

- Feelings of hopelessness, depression, and numbness. (Cynthia felt nothing she did had any impact on Martin's behavior.)

In the same way that a lack of knowledge and myths in the media about sex addiction make it harder for men to ask for help, their partners have unhelpful beliefs that hold back recovery too, including:

- *It's my fault.* The partner believes that if she had been sexier, more sexually liberated, more understanding, attentive (the list is endless), she could have headed off the crisis. This is a natural reaction to the helplessness many women feel after discovery. They hope by taking all the blame, they can regain control. After all, this false reasoning goes, if I change, he'll change, and everything will be okay. With most relationship problems, this can indeed be a way forward. However, if your partner is truly a sex addict, your actions will have little or no effect on his behavior. Even if your partner is only abusing pornography, he has to take responsibility for his behavior.

- *If he looks at porn, he doesn't love me.* This kind of "all-or-nothing" or "black-and-white" thinking increases the stakes and does not take into consideration the complexity of human feelings.

- *I'm not good enough.* Personalizing everything is another way of trying to regain control, although in a self-destructive way. A man's use of pornography probably says more about his childhood and his inability to deal with stress and anxiety than it does about his partner.

- *All men are animals.* Overgeneralizations and magnification of the problem undermine coping skills and encourage panicked, rather than thought-out reactions.

- *He looked at the waitress; he must have found her attractive.* Jumping to conclusions or drawing from one area of your life to make an ironclad case for another, for example, "He's tired and irritable, so he must be lying again," makes recovery harder and discounts any positives left in a relationship.

## WHAT TO DO IF YOU DISCOVER YOUR PARTNER IS ABUSING PORNOGRAPHY OR USING PROSTITUTES

Although every situation is different, there are some common strategies for moving forward either together or apart:

1. Don't make any long-term decisions while you're still in shock, especially about whom to tell and whether to stay or go.

2. Find out what really has been happening in your relationship. Keep calm and try not to condemn too much, as shame will make your partner clam up and hold back information. Remember, it will probably take time to get full disclosure, so keep the lines of communication open.

3. Take care of yourself. Think carefully about digging for specific or graphic details as these could put pictures into your head, which might hamper your recovery. When you feel compelled to find something out, step back and ask yourself why. Are you trying to punish yourself? Are you looking for a magic solution that will take everything back to how it was? How realistic is this?

4. Read books and consult websites from appropriate organizations like Sex Addicts Anonymous and Sex and Love Addicts Anonymous. Seek to understand the difference between using, abusing, and becoming addicted to pornography, adult chat lines, etc. It is important not to minimize your discovery; however, exaggerating the evidence is equally unhelpful.

5. Decision time for your relationship will be later than you expect. This should come only when you truly know what you're committing to or what you're walking away from. In this way, you will make an informed decision and one to which you can stick.

6. Seek professional help. If your partner's behavior is compulsive, he should be in some sort of treatment program, but you will also need support either from your own therapist or a couple's therapist. If it's you who is using or abusing pornography, there is advice in the exercise section.

7. Do not expect too much change too quickly. It will have taken years for your partner's problems to take hold, so do not expect the damage to be redeemed overnight.

## RECOVERING FROM SEXUAL ABUSE

In this chapter thus far I've covered how discovering your partner's affair or use of pornography can make you angry and make it difficult to act as a team. The third category of common problems that make solving sexual problems harder is past sexual abuse and is far more complex than the others. Although the partners of people who have been abused are sympathetic and want to help, they also feel helpless and frustrated, and frustration can turn to anger. Meanwhile, the person who has been abused has plenty of anger herself or himself, but often it is focused inward. All too often, abuse is such a painful subject that it becomes an off-limits topic with each partner on a different side of the divide.

Lynne, whom we met earlier in the last chapter, revealed that a group of boys she'd hung out with when she was fifteen had taken advantage of her. "I was a cocky kid. Always mouthing off about this or that, and I suppose I came across as more knowledgeable and experienced about sex than I really was. I wanted to impress the boys; I wanted to be liked. One boy dared me to go with him into the public restroom at the park." Lynne began to cry.

My approach when people reveal abuse is not to push for details or encourage them to "relive" the experience in the hope of exorcising the pain, as this seems needlessly painful (and I don't think it really helps). Instead, I allow them enough time to tell me what they choose.

"The other boys followed us in, but it was mainly one boy."

However, in order to understand the impact the past has on the present, and on a person's sex life and, in particular, on today, I ask for the headlines.

"What did he do?" I asked.

"He tried to rape me, but I struggled, made a lot of noise, and they got frightened and ran away."

"Did you tell anybody?"

"Nobody, until this week. We made love, and I was lying in Michael's arms and it sort of tumbled out."

## The Abuse Triangle

Abuse brings up all sorts of powerful feelings. Sometimes, in my counseling room, it feels like the emotions are bouncing off the walls or closing in on us. This is probably because abusers ignore boundaries between what is acceptable behavior and what is not, or overwhelm the protective barriers of victims. Therefore, the painful feelings know no boundaries either and can attach somewhere they don't belong. The best way to understand this phenomenon is to think of a triangle.

When Lynne confided in Michael, he had taken on the role of rescuer. "I told her that there was nothing to be ashamed about, and it wasn't her fault," he said.

So far, so good. However, the abuse triangle is never very stable. The couple lived in a small town, and Michael knew Lynne's abuser.

"I got really angry about what he'd done to Lynne and wanted to punch his lights out," he told me.

At this point, everyone on the triangle had switched places. Michael became the aggressor, the "abuser," in search of vigilante violence, which

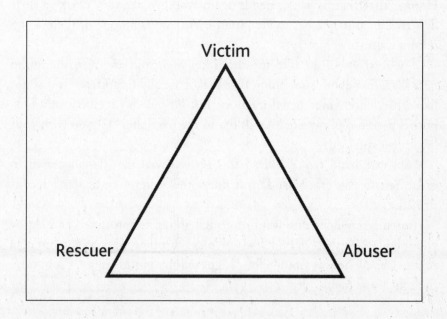

is never the answer. Lynne got terribly agitated because she was worried everything would come out and sprang to her abuser's defense. In other words, she had become the "rescuer" and her abuser had become the "victim."

In other cases, the abuse triangle can be even more insidious. I had worked with Rosemary, forty-eight, and her partner in the aftermath of his affair and guided them through the seven steps toward a renewed relationship, but something was holding Rosemary back.

"Thomas and I have a much better sex life. We talk more than ever before. I got a promotion. Life should be good, but it's like I'm wearing a black cloak."

"What kind of cloak?" I asked. "A fashionable poncho?"

"No. One that goes floor to ceiling with a hood."

I have to admit that I was puzzled. I would not have expected something so all enveloping at this stage. So we tried replacing negative images with positives ones but with only limited success. When Rosemary found out about Thomas's infidelity, she leaned heavily on her friends but, over time, became embarrassed about the amount of support she needed and just how much they knew about her and her weaknesses, so she withdrew. Hoping that sharing with friends again would make the "cloak" a little lighter, I encouraged her to accept an invitation from one of them to go out for a drink.

The next week, she told me about her night out and how she found herself talking about something that she'd basically forgotten. "It was not like a suddenly remembered memory, but I'd put this incident in a box, buried it, and told myself, "It's all the in the past" and "Get on with your life," she explained.

"On one hand, you'd buried this box so well that it had ceased to exist. Yet on the other hand, you knew the secret coordinates," I confirmed.

Rosemary nodded and went on to tell about her protected and happy childhood. "My best friend had an older brother who was a bit of a rogue. I knew he was trouble, but I ignored my gut instincts. I suppose I thought I was invincible."

At eighteen, Rosemary had been out for a drink with a group of friends and bumped into this man. He joined the group and at the end of the evening offered to give Rosemary a lift home. She could have phoned her dad or taken the bus home but she accepted. "I found him rather exciting and dangerous," she remembered.

However, she got more than she bargained for.

"He stopped the car in the middle of nowhere and switched off the engine," Rosemary said. 'You've got two choices: you can either go down on this,' he said pointing to his bulge in his pants, 'or get out of the car and find your own way home.' I thought of all the talks from Dad about 'putting myself at risk' and 'being stupid,' and I didn't want to upset everybody so instead of getting out, I took the other option. The next morning, I told myself 'nobody got hurt' and 'I'm stronger than this,' and I went off to college as if nothing had happened."

However, something had happened.

"Over the years, I've become quite callous. If they want somebody fired, they always ask me to do the deed. I'm rational, unemotional, and get the job done. I suppose, I thought, deep down, that if I could deal with that abuse then surely they can cope with being fired. So many times, I've told colleagues to pull themselves together and stop bringing their private stuff to work. I've been a complete bitch."

In effect, Rosemary had been perilously close to abusing her colleagues. Certainly, I considered her lack of regard for her needs as abusive toward herself.

"When I discovered Thomas's affair, I didn't even go in to work late," she said. "I could cope. No sick days for me. Nothing would hurt me, how stupid. Because I wound up making myself ill and ended up in hospital with colitis."

## What to Do if Your Partner Reveals Abuse

Although most of the help, quite rightly, is focused on the "victim" of the abuse, it is equally important that his or her partner gets support too. It is horrible to discover that someone you love has been through terrible experiences and the story can hang like a cloud over your relationship. In some cases, the partner finds his loving sex has been tainted by past abusive sex or feels like the abuser for suggesting anything more than a kiss and a cuddle. (Remember, the abuse triangle is never solid and all the positions can change very easily.) If this sounds familiar, here are some guidelines for coping in the aftermath of your partner's disclosure.

- *Report your anger rather than act it out.* By this I mean tell your partner, "I feel angry about . . ." but don't seek revenge on your partner's behalf. At the other extreme, don't keep your feelings bottled up as this could be perceived as being angry with your partner or being rejecting.

- *Take your lead from your partner.* Go along with your partner's approach to dealing with the problem. It is terribly important for victims of abuse to be in charge. After all, they certainly were not in control when the abuse happened. So if your partner wants to report the abuser to the police or confront the relevant family member or let the matter drop, that's up to him or her. It's fine to give your opinion and help your partner think through the consequences, but the decision is not yours to make. Your job is, ultimately, to support your partner.

- *Be patient and ready to listen.* It will take your partner time to unload all the pain, and talking will bring up fresh memories. The journey can take years rather than weeks and months, especially as some victims will not seek legal redress until after their parents have died. This is typical because the victim feels they would be, in some way, "letting them down" or "shaming them," or causing them to blame themselves for not "protecting them" from the abuser.

## How to Move Forward

This is a huge subject, and there are many excellent books on recovering from sexual abuse, so I will only focus on reducing the impact the disclosure has on your relationship and your lovemaking.

- *Deal with the blame.* Many victims feel that they were in some way to blame. Lynne was angry with herself for being "a know-it-all" and that she "had it coming to me." Rosemary felt it was her fault for accepting the car ride home. This is nonsense. In many cases, abusers are adults in positions of power, and the victim has little or no control. Even when the abuser is a near contemporary, the victim is not a clairvoyant nor has the ability to predict the secret intentions of the abuser.

- Be aware that many abusers rationalize themselves into the victim role by blaming the object of their abuse, e.g., "She egged me on" or "He wanted it." (We're back to the abuse triangle being profoundly unstable.) Sadly, many victims take these groundless accusations as the truth. Fortunately, talking about what happened exposes all of the negative self-talk associated with abuse and any self-justification from the abusers, which has been internalized. Slowly over time, it is possible to have a more balanced view and put blame where it truly belongs.

- *Frame the problems in the "now."* It is always better to focus on how the abuse is still affecting you today than wishing you could change what happened yesterday. Neil, forty-three, had been repeatedly forced to have sex by his long-term foster father, who had abused most of the children in his care. Neil came to counseling with his second wife, Alison, not because of sexual problems—in fact, their lovemaking was the glue of their relationship—but because of repeated arguments and his "moodiness." Neil had disclosed the abuse early into their relationship. "I don't know why, because I never told my first wife, but perhaps I thought Alison would understand; perhaps I knew keeping it secret ruined my first marriage."

  However, he had not told Alison much more than those headlines so she did not understand the full impact the abuse had on him today. Over a period of six months in counseling, Neil explained that he got angry when Alison shut the bedroom door, not because he was being difficult, as Alison had thought, but because Neil's abuser shut the bedroom door so his foster mother could not hear what was happening. He explained that he did not have an irrational fear of bananas as

Alison had thought. If he had "misbehaved" as a child, Neil would be sent up to bed with no dinner and just a banana for energy, which would be the time when his foster father was most likely to strike. Once Alison understood the overhang from Neil's past abuse, many of the triggers for their current arguments disappeared.

- *Take control.* Look at how past abuse affects your sex life today. Unsurprisingly, Rosemary was not particularly keen on giving oral sex. "I do it because Thomas enjoys it, and I want to give him pleasure." This is hardly the foundation for passionate lovemaking. So I broke down the ingredients that brought back the strongest memories for Rosemary.

   "If Thomas holds my head, that puts me straight back into the car," she explained.

   Thomas had not been aware of this and readily agreed not to touch her head if she performed oral sex on him.

   Next, I helped Rosemary take control and set the pace of how fast oral sex progressed. What would happen if she licked around the penis, tantalizing all the most sensitive points (like underneath the head) and slowly building up the sexual tension, until finally *she* chose the moment to put Thomas's penis into her mouth? In this way, she would actively be *giving* Thomas oral sex and would be completely in control. The couple tried this experiment, and Rosemary found she could detach this aspect of making love from her past trauma.

- *Become a survivor.* When abuse is buried or forgotten, it is not possible to challenge all the distorted thinking or ease the pain. Under these circumstances, the person who suffered the abuse will feel like a victim. However, once they accept that this abuse really did happen (rather than pretending or wishing it did not), they can begin to understand both the ways that the abuse has affected them *and* how they have can overcome or transcend the trauma. Sometimes, people even discover it has made them stronger or more sensitive to other people's distress. In this way, they move from being a victim to being a survivor. Ultimately, this is a better place to be, but it takes time and hard work to get there.

## SOMETHING TO SLEEP ON

**In summary, remember:**

- Affairs put the spotlight on a couple's sex life and help them break through excuses like "It's not that important" or "We're too tired," so they can reinvent how they make love.

- Men and women have different attitudes toward pornography, and every couple has to decide for themselves what is acceptable and what is not. Unfortunately, when men are depressed, they often use porn to "medicate" their feelings, which in the long run can lead to serious relationship problems.

- Sexual abuse, even in the past, will cast a shadow on the present. However, if you can work as a team, it's easier to heal and move from victim to survivor.

# SEX ED

### EXERCISE 21   HOW TO STOP A PORN HABIT FROM GETTING OUT OF CONTROL

Internet porn has the potential to be highly addictive, so if you're concerned about the amount of time consumed by pornography, the effect on your relationship or your own self-esteem, take control with the following steps.

1. **Don't go cold turkey.** You have probably vowed never to use porn again and maybe even stopped for a while, but slowly slipped back into using it. This is because stopping alone is not enough. You need to understand what underpins your porn usage.

2. **Monitor your consumption.** There are key things to note:

229

- What are the triggers?
- How do you feel when using pornography?
- How much time has passed?
- How do you feel afterward?

When I did this exercise with Shane, he identified his triggers were "feeling sorry for myself," "I deserve this for working hard," "loneliness," "an aching feeling inside," and "celebration after hearing some good news." The feelings he felt during consumption were "trance-like," "out of body," and "similar to paralysis"—all signs that he was using pornography to anesthetize, or self-medicate. Shane reported that he was using pornography about five or six hours a week and afterward felt "resigned, shameful, and pathetic."

3. **Tackle the triggers.** Think about alternatives for dealing with triggers rather than going to the Internet. If you are feeling stressed and need to unwind, what about phoning a friend or talking to your partner about what happened? If there are particular vulnerable times (like a weekend night), plan ahead and find other ways to occupy yourself. What diversion tactics could you use?

4. **Live the feelings.** When it comes to difficult feelings, like sadness, feeling sorry for yourself, and loneliness, there are three ways to cope. The first is to block them out (which you have been doing with pornography). The second is to divert your feelings (for example, switching on the TV and distracting yourself). The third is to look the feelings directly in the eye. Acknowledge them (I'm feeling. . .), and accept them (Everybody feels. . . from time to time) instead of trying to rationalize them away or ignore them. Next, allow yourself to experience the feelings (just sit quietly and see if you can bear them). In my experience, the feelings are magnified when you block them out. When they are "lived," they are normally unpleasant but not as scary as you expected. (Shane was

amazed to discover that rather than plunging into depression, as he had feared, the depressed feelings passed. There was another bonus—no more morning-after regrets from a night of Internet pornography.)

5. **Listen to the feelings and make the changes.** Our feelings normally have something important to tell us. For example, Shane's were telling him that he needed to spend less time at work and more time socializing so he could find a partner. Unfortunately, we don't always like the message and rationalize it away. ("I've got to work hard or my business will suffer.") Sometimes the message is inconvenient, frightening, or threatens to turn your life upside down. ("I'm bored and unfulfilled by my sex life with my partner, but if I say anything she will be upset and angry.") It is as if you are a square peg trying to fit into a round hole (and self-medicating to cope with the pain). What would be better: facing the problem head on and changing, or continuing to block out the feelings and maintain the status quo?

6. **Be realistic.** If the problems are deep-rooted, for example, abuse when you were a child, it might be too painful to listen to your feelings without professional support. If you have been using pornography in a compulsive manner for a long time or if your life has become chaotic or your behavior destructive, you should also consider entering a twelve-step program or joining a support group.

### EXERCISE 22   DEFINING A HEALTHY SEXUALITY

Whether you are struggling with a porn habit and considering where the boundary between acceptable and unacceptable behavior lie, or thinking about asking your partner to experiment with a particular sexual practice, it is useful to have a positive benchmark against which to test yourself. So ask yourself the following questions:

- Does this activity build my self-esteem?

- Are there any negative consequences?

- Will I be hurting my partner or other people?

- What would my partner say if he or she found out?

- Taking into consideration my answers to the first four questions, what is acceptable sexual behavior?

- Taking into consideration my answers to the first four questions, what is *not* acceptable sexual behavior?

- What activities might be sliding down a slippery slope, i.e., the acceptable behaviors that might encourage me to cross the line into unacceptable territory?

When I did this exercise with Shane, he decided that *healthy* sexuality included "sex with feelings, consensual sex, and asking for sex" while *unhealthy* sexuality included "pestering for sex, paying a prostitute, and pornography." For a slippery slope activity, he decided to include "going for a massage, even if I keep my pants on" and that it would be better if he hired a male masseuse rather than a female.

# Conclusion

Good sex is about good communication. The first step to becoming more sensual and improving your love life is taking a break from sex and learning to talk and listen better. Doing so ignites giving and receiving in the bedroom and turns you from two bored or frustrated individuals into a loving team. Ultimately, it is never too late to change and have a passionate and plentiful sex life. All you need is a little knowledge, patience, and the belief that you can reignite the spark again.

Although you have learned a lot about your own sexuality through my program, the main benefits are intended to affect you as a couple. So if your partner has doubts about getting on board, what should you do?

- Examine how you have presented the program. Is it as criticism or an opportunity to promote change? Tell your partner how much you love him or her, talk about the pleasures of your current lovemaking, and how you'd like to build on these achievements.

- Are you using this book as a secret test? If you're angry and resentful and are using your partner's reaction to this book as a way of deciding whether to stay or go, your feelings will leak through your tone of voice and body language. Under these circumstances, your partner will be worried that trying and failing will become a stick with which to beat him or her.

- Instead of working on your relationship, work on yourself. The first approach risks gridlock, as it suggests that your partner needs to change before anything can improve. However, working on yourself will break the gridlock because any changes you make will have a positive effect on your partner's behavior.

Every couple needs to find their own pace through this program, so do not be discouraged if outside events or personal fears make progress difficult.

## MY BEST PARTING ADVICE

I believe that ultimately every couple knows best what is right for them and their love life. Although I have offered a general program, it can be tailored to suit your particular needs, situation, and goals. If something is not right for you, skip that part or figure out a way to alter it, so it is. However, I recommend that every couple puts a temporary ban on intercourse and follows the first four weeks of the program, A Month of Sensuality. It is vital to undo the myth that a cuddle should lead to intercourse. If you need longer than a week for a particular phase, take it. This is not a race. Stay with the exercise until both of you feel ready to continue.

Whatever happens, keep talking. This is especially important when you feel blocked. After all, talking about your problems and your fears is half the battle of solving them.

Andrew G. Marshall
www.andrewgmarshall.com

# Appendix

# Putting the Spark
# Back into Your Relationship

At the heart of this book is a ten-week program that allows you to return back to relationship basics, begin to touch each other in a sensual way rather than just sexual, and build up the levels of intimacy until you are ready to experiment and take risks. This appendix serves as your easy reference to the program's exercises.

## A MONTH OF SENSUALITY
### (See Chapter Four)

A Month of Sexuality encompasses four weeks. For each of the exercises, start with fifteen minutes of touching and then switch places for fifteen minutes of being touched. As the weeks progress, add ingredients.

**Week One**  Cuddling and Sensual Touching

Experiment with different ways of touching your partner, e.g., a firm back rub or light and teasing. Avoid the genitals.

**Week Two**  Kissing

Stay with sensual touch but find new places to kiss your partner and in different ways (butterfly, wet, and nibbling). Avoid the genitals. Finish with a lingering kiss on your partner's mouth and look into each other's eyes.

**Week Three**  Advanced Sensual Touching

Stay with sensual touching and kissing, but add in new sensations by caressing each other with different fabrics and implements. Finish by showing each other how you like your breasts or nipples to be stimulated and guiding your partner's hand so he or she knows how to replicate these pleasures.

**Week Four**  Being Sexual Together

Stay with sensual touching, kissing, and your favorite elements of advanced sensual touching, and finish the session by masturbating yourselves in front of each other. Pay attention to how your partner likes to be touched, so you can incorporate that knowledge into future lovemaking.

## TWO WEEKS OF WICKEDNESS
### (See Chapter Five)

**Week Five**  Show and Tell

Take a long look at yourself in the mirror—long enough to move past your normal reaction to your naked body. Say aloud or write down what you like about your body. Next, examine your genitals, in detail, as if you've never seen them before. What positive things have you discovered? Later in the week, stand naked in front of the mirror with your partner. Tell him or her what you like about your body. Show him or her your hidden or less visible parts. Look carefully at how your partner handles his or her genitals, as this will provide clues for how you might touch your partner. Finally, give compliments to each other.

**Week Six**  Focus on Arousal

After five minutes of sensual touching, the first partner begins to explore the other's genitals and then slowly mixes genital touching with whole-body touching. This exercise is not about arousing your partner, so don't worry if at the beginning the penis is not erect or the vagina is not lubricated. This week is about making love to the whole person. Finish with a cuddle rather than an orgasm.

## TWO WEEKS OF VARIETY
### (See Chapter Six)

**Week Seven**   Different Strokes

Start with the usual sensual touching and kissing to get into the mood for being sexual together. After a while, once the touchee is in the mood, he or she should start to touch his or her genitals. The toucher watches and then puts his or her hands over the touchee's and shadows the style and type of masturbation exhibited. Finally, the toucher takes over and masturbates the touchee. Afterward, switch places.

**Week Eight**   Oral Sex

Begin this exercise by taking a shower or bath together and thoroughly washing each other's genitals. The toucher builds from sensual touching to fondling genitals and graduates to using tongue, lips, and mouth to give pleasure. Finally, the toucher brings the touchee to orgasm either orally or manually (or with a vibrator). Afterward, switch places, with the toucher becoming the touchee.

## TWO WEEKS OF EXPANSION
### (See Chapter Seven)

**Week Nine**   Partner A Chooses

Flip a coin and decide who goes first and takes charge of your sex life. Everything from your past styles of lovemaking is on the menu again, including intercourse, but Partner A can come up with something new that has not been done before or not for a long time. Partner B will give this idea his or her full consideration and try to find a way of incorporating it either in full or in part. It is worth noting that this is an experiment, and agreeing to try something is not tantamount to committing to this activity for life. Afterward, discuss what you enjoyed and what elements you would like to continue using.

**Week Ten** Partner B Chooses

It is Partner B's chance to introduce something new into the relationship and for Partner A to try to embrace the idea. This is your chance to show your partner something new about your sexuality. How could you invite your partner on your journey of discovery? Finish with another discussion about how you can use this new knowledge.

# About the Author

**Andrew G. Marshall** is a marital therapist with close to thirty years' experience who has written the international bestseller, *I Love You but I'm Not in Love with You: Seven Steps to Saving Your Relationship* as well as ten other books on relationships, including *I Love You but You Always Put Me Last: Why the Kids-First Approach to Parenting Is Hurting Your Marriage—and the Proven Plan to Restore Balance; My Wife Doesn't Love Me Anymore: The Love Coach Guide to Winning Her Back; How Can I Ever Trust You Again? Infidelity from Discovery to Recovery in Seven Steps; Learn to Love Yourself Enough: Seven Steps to Improving Self-Esteem in All Your Relationships; Help Your Partner Say "Yes": Seven Steps to Achieving Better Cooperation and Communication;* and *Heal and Move On: Seven Steps to Recovering from a Breakup.*

Andrew's work has been translated into twenty languages. He has trained with RELATE (the UK's leading couple's counseling charity) and has a private practice offering counseling, workshops, and inspirational talks in London.

Visit the author at www.andrewgmarshall.com
Follow him on twitter: @andrewgmarshall